Instructor's Manual and Test Bank to Accompany

The Moral of the Story

An Introduction to Ethics

Second Edition

Nina Rosenstand
San Diego State University

Mayfield Publishing Company
Mountain View, California
London • Toronto

International Standard Book Number: 1-55934-649-3

Manufactured in the United States of America
10 9 8 7 6 5 4 3 2 1

Mayfield Publishing Company
1280 Villa Street
Mountain View, California 94041

CONTENTS

PART II   TEST BANK: OBJECTIVE AND ESSAY QUESTIONS

PREFACE

In writing this manual accompanying the second edition of *The Moral of the Story*, I've set out to accomplish two things: (1) to provide you with a "road map" to the text, including suggestions for further class discussions, and (2) to make available to you a set of suggested test questions. Part I of this manual, Class Presentation Material, covers organization of the textbook and contains an overview and specific suggestions for each chapter. Part II, Test Bank: Objective and Essay Questions, contains a bank of true/false, multiple-choice, and essay/study questions for each chapter.

The Moral of the Story is an introduction to ethical theory, written primarily for college courses covering subjects such as *Introduction to Philosophy: Values*, *Introduction to Ethics*, and *Moral Problems*. In addition, *The Moral of the Story* contains sections on philosophy and literature in a broad sense (including film) that may be used as a supplementary text in courses in *Philosophy and Literature* and *Philosophy and Film*.

While many textbooks in value-theory/ethics present problems of social importance for students to discuss, such as abortion, euthanasia, and capital punishment, I personally find that it is better for students to be introduced to basic ethical theory before they plunge into discussions involving moral judgments. The main focus of this book is thus an overview of some classical and modern approaches to ethical theory such as ethical relativism, egoism, utilitarianism, deontology, and virtue-theory.

However, since I believe that a full understanding of any ethical theory is only possible through the application of that theory to specific cases, I have chosen numerous examples to illustrate the theories in question. Over the years I have experimented with showing films and reading fiction as part of a philosophy course, and I have come to believe that one of the best ways to illustrate ethical theory is through the use of fictional narratives. My own students usually respond very well to this approach, and I hope yours will, too. The positive response to the first edition of *The Moral of the Story* indicates that many other instructors find this approach stimulating. I find it personally to be a particularly gratifying experience to use literature/film in conjunction with philosophy in the classroom. This combination of theory and practice is usually novel to the student. I hope you may find this experience both refreshing and rewarding, too.

Incidentally, just in case any student should misunderstand my meaning, you might mention that the Noel Coward motto on the front leaf is intended as ironic. The line is made hugely fun of by the three main characters of the play: the woman and her two lovers, a playwright and a painter living in a *ménage a trois* (supposedly platonic) in an artist's apartment in Paris. Ernest Lubitch made it into a film in 1933 with Gary Cooper, Frederich March, Miriam Hopkins, and Edward Everett Horton (speaking the quoted line) and it is still worth watching. You may want to discuss with your students whether or not the quote has merit, regardless of Coward's intention.

PART I
Class Presentation Materials

A BRIEF OVERVIEW OF THE TEXT

The second edition of *The Moral of the Story* is divided into three major sections. Part 1 introduces the topic of ethics, morals, and values, and places the phenomenon of storytelling within the context of cross-cultural moral education and discussion. Part 2 examines the conduct theories of ethichal realativism, psychological and ethical egoism, utilitarianism, and Kantian deontology, and explores the concepts of personhood, rights, and justice. Part 3 focuses on the subject of virtue theory and contains chapters on Socrates and Plato, Aristotle, contemporary virtue theories in American and Continental philosophy, and gender theory. In addition the topic of virtues and values in the context of world religions is explored, and the virtues of compassion and gratitude are examined in detail. The book concludes with a short chapter on the moral importance of storytelling.

Primary Readings

The Moral of the Story contains extensive citations from classical texts; in addition, this edition has one or more *Primary Readings* attached to each chapter. These short text excerpts have been selected as companion readings to be studied in conjunction with the chapter in question; most of these excerpts are from classical passages in ethical theory; however, if a text has been thoroughly discussed and illustrated with quotes within the theoretical chapter, I have opted for a less well known excerpt instead (for example, Chapter 6, which introduces Kant's deontology, has a discussion of the categorical imperative that includes a long quote from *The Grounding* (*Groundwork*); as the Primary Reading I have selected a section from Kant's *Metaphysics of Morals* on lying, rather than have the students read about the categorical imperative twice.)

The Primary Readings follow immediately after each chapter and are indicated with an icon. Each Primary Reading has a set of study questions to facilitate the class discussion and possibly serve as elements in essay questions and term papers (see Part II, the Test Bank).

In additon to including Primary Readings, this edition also has a new chapter structure to facilitate the use of Narratives: You will now find the Narratives attached to the relevant chapters. Chapter 1, "Who Cares about Ethics," has a new discussion of ethics on the Internet, and now includes *Jurassic Park* as the Narrative dealing with the ethics of science. Chapter 2, "Stories with Morals," has been edited, and a new discussion of storytelling as a method of understanding oneself has been added. This chapter also has Primary Readings from Plato and Aristotle focusing on the value of drama; the narrative selection includes Euripides' *The Bacchants* and Tarantino's *Pulp Fiction*. Chapter 3, "Ethical Relativism," has an expanded discussion of multiculturalism; the Primary Readings consist of excerpts from Benedict's "Anthropology and the Abnormal," and an argument for multiculturalism by Bhikhu Parekh. The Narratives include an expanded summary of *Do the Right Thing,* and a new addition: excerpts from Alice Walker's *Possessing the Secret of Joy.* Chapter 4, "Myself or Others?" has an expanded discussion of psychological egoism; the Primary Reading is from Ayn Rand's "The Ethics of Emergencies;" an added Narrative is from the film *Hero. Madame Bovary* now is represented by an excerpt as well as a summary. Chapter 5, "Using Your Reason, Part I, Utilitarianism," has an expanded section on John Stuart Mill, and one on Harriet Taylor. In addition there is a new box on the issue of animal suffering. The Primary Readings are from Bentham's *Introduction to the Principles of*

Morals and Legislation, and John Stuart Mill's *Utilitarianism.* The excerpt from Dostoyevsky's *The Brothers Karamazov* has been expanded, and an excerpt added to LeGuin's "The Ones Who Walk Away from Omelas." A new Narrative summary is the film *Outbreak.* Chapter 6, "Kant's Deontology," contains additional material on the nature of reason, including animal intelligence. The Primary Reading is from Kant's *Metaphysics of Morals.* A new Narrative summarizes *The Bridges of Madison County.* Chapter 7, "Personhood, Rights, and Justice" contains some of the discussion from the first edition Chapter 14 on personhood, but is otherwise all new, exploring the concepts of justice and tights, from libertarian to liberal viewpoints. Issues discussed include the topics of bioethics, and the death penalty. Thinkers featured include John Hospers, Ayn Rand, John Rawls, Marilyn Friedman and others. The Primary Readings are from the United Nations Declaration of Human Rights, and from Rawls's "Justice as Fairness;" the Narratives are the film *Blade Runner* (from the first edition, Chapter 20), and the shorth story "The Jigsaw Man." Chapter 8, "Socrates, Plato, and the Good Life," now has a section exploring the political background behind the death of Socrates. The Primary Reading is from Plato's *Apology,* and the Narratives are the film *A Man for All Seasons,* Plato's Myth of the Cave, the short story "The Store of the Worlds," and *Cyrano de Bergerac.* Chapter 9, "Aristotle's Virtue Theory," has very few changes from the first edition. The Primary Reading is from the Nichomachean Ethics; a new Narrative is the Greek myth, "The Fall of Icarus." Chapter 10, "Modern Perspectives," (Chapter 11 in the first edition) continues the focus on virtue ethics with an expanded discussion of modern virtue theory; the second part of the chapter which introduces the Continental tradition has a new introductory section on Emmanuel Levinas. The Primary Readings are a short Kierkegaard section, and an excerpt from an interview with Levinas. A new Narrative is the film *A Few Good Men.* Chapter 11, "Different Gender, Different Ethic?" is a rewritten version of Chapter 16 in the first edition, with additional material reflecting some current issues in the gender debate. The Primary Reading excerpt is from Gilligan's *In a Different Voice.* New Narratives are the classic *A Doll's House* and Esquivel's *Like Water for Chocolate.* Chapter 12, "Virtues, Values, and Religion," is an expanded and reorganized version of the previous Chapter 10. Primary Readings are short quotes from scriptures or moral laws of the traditions represented in this chapter; new Narratives include Isaac Bashevis Singer's "A Piece of Advice," the Native American myth "White Buffalo Woman," the Arabic folktale "Test of Friendship," and the African folktale "The Quality of Friendship." Chapter 13, "Case Studies in Virtue," is a virtually unchanged version of Chapter 12 from the first edition. The Primary Reading is from Lin Yutang's *The Importance of Living,* and new Narratives include the film *Eat, Drink, Man, Woman,* and the film, *Grand Canyon.* The concluding Chapter 14 is a short excursion into the social importance of storytelling, containing elements from the concluding chapter of the first edition. There are no Primary Readings, but two Narratives conclude the book: An episode from the television series *Star Trek:* "Voyager," and Salman Rushdie's novel *Haroun and the Sea of Stories.*

Some Suggestions on How to Use the Narratives

My intention with the Narratives is the same as in the first edition: For the instructor to choose one or two stories per chapter to discuss with her or his students; generally I have included two or more, because I find that there are so many good stories to talk about, and I would like the instructor to have a choice, and perhaps vary the selection from semester to semester (which is what I do myself). It is not my intention that you should go through all these stories with the students. Except in the case where *The Moral of the Story* is used specifically in a class focusing on literature and philosophy, few philosophy instructors will have enough time set aside to go into detail with more than a few Narratives; however, the book is designed so that you can choose one or two stories to illustrate each theoretical problem.

The Narratives have been chosen from a wide variety of cross-cultural sources. I wish to emphasize that from a literary and artistic point of view these summaries of course don't do the originals justice; a story worth experiencing, be it a novel, a short story, or a film, can't be reduced to a mere plot-outline or an excerpt and still retain all of its essence. Furthermore, there is usually more to the story than the bare bones of a moral problem, and in writing the summaries I have had to disregard much of the the richness of story and character development. Nevertheless I have chosen the summary and/or excerpt format in order to be able to discuss a number of different stories and genres as they relate to specific issues in ethics; and since I believe it is important to show that there is a cross-cultural, historic tradition of exploring moral problems through telling a story, I have opted for a broad selection of narrative outlines.

Not all themes in the book are illustrated by narrative examples—that would have been an overwhelming task; however, if you find that a theme should be emphasized further by adding an outline of a Narrative you are familiar with, I would certainly appreciate your suggestion.

Each Narrative or group of Narratives has a few study questions at the end. These questions are not intended to exhaust the discussion topic, but rather to get a discussion started.

Each Narrative is marked with an icon signifying whether the story is a novel, a short story, a film, a television show, or a play; several of the stories are marked with several different icons: the first icon will signify which story-format the outline is based on, and the following icon(s) will tell if there are other formats to this story. Example: Shakespeare's *Othello* is marked by the icon for "play," but carries a secondary icon signifying "film." Only the most important alternative media versions of a story are marked by secondary icons; thus, if a well-known film is based on a book that has not had the same impact, only the film icon will be displayed.

I usually discuss the story *after* going over the theoretical chapter with my students, but you may want to incorporate the story into the theoretical discussion itself.

There are, of course, many other ways in which stories and ethical theory can be brought together: one might, for instance, select one or two short stories or films in their original format for class discussion; I am hoping that you will indeed select a few stories—a novel, a short story, or a video—for your students to experience firsthand.[1] However, the outlines are written so that a first-hand experience should not be necessary for a discussion of the problem presented by the story; the outlines give the students just enough information to engage in a discussion of the moral problem presented. It is my hope that some students might actually become inspired to seek out the originals on their own; I am happy to report this being the case with many of my own students.

Since space is limited, I have not been able to include more than a sampling of stories, and I readily admit that the criteria of choice are my own; I personally find them interesting as illustrations, and effective in a classroom context where students of today come from many different cultural backgrounds. They are selected on the basis of their clarity in presenting moral problems, and not from any evaluation of their quality as enduring classics, nor from any grand plan of systematically representing all aspects of world literature. I am fully aware that you might choose other stories, and even choose completely different ethical problems to be illustrated, and I am happy to say that the second edition incorporates several suggestions of new narratives from colleagues as well as students. I would be delighted to hear from you how this new selection of stories might be improved. Please feel free to contact me by e-mail (rosensta@mail.sdsu.edu). Most of the narratives are available in libraries, bookstores, and video/laser disc rental stores.

While most students relate immediately to the idea of applying questions of value and moral issues to stories, you should be prepared that there are a few students who have never been exposed to the idea that a story may be telling more than its actual plot. I have found, through experience, that the idea of symbolism or metaphor in a story is completely unfamiliar to a small percentage of students, and before embarking on an ethical analysis of the stories in this book you might do well if you spend a few minutes explaining to the students that stories have several levels: a story-line level, and any number of levels where the author "speaks between the lines," addressing psychological, social, or political issues through his or her characters. In much popular fiction these levels tend to be at a minimum, while in what is known as "higher literature" such levels may be numerous.

For a viewpoint that is squarely opposed to this approach of using stories in ethics you may want to examine a book by Peter Thorpe, *Why Literature Is Bad for You* (Chicago: Nelson-Hall, 1980). In his book Thorpe argues that authors and literature professors are a small and mentally rather deviant minority that doesn't represent the moral values of the majority: they oversimplify moral problems, make their readers and students lazy and self-centered, and make them tolerant of incompetence. Above all, Thorpe says authors have invented the generation gap, which didn't exist before they started writing about it. In addition, Thorpe seems to believe novels should be read mainly as plot outlines, if at all. As you can probably tell, I disagree with most of his arguments, but the book is provocative and entertaining.

In the next sextion on Course Material there will be listings of a few additional narratives, should you wish to explore the subject further with your class.

---

[1] Please note that copyright restrictions apply to the showing of videos in a classroom situation. Your school should be able to inform you of current copyright regulations.

Boxes in the Instructor's Manual

In this manual you will find several boxes titled "Author's Tip." They contain suggestions concerning the class discussion material, or tidbit information that I found too esoteric to be included in the text, but which you might want to convey to your students anyway. They are by no means a listing of all posssible discussion topics, but merely suggestions for further discussion of themes explored in the text.

Alternative Teaching Scenarios

The Moral of the Story is designed to accommodate several different teaching scenarios. Its 14 chapters are designed to fill the teaching needs of one semester. Here I have outlined strategy options for (1) a semester schedule and (2) a quarter schedule.

One Semester (15–18 weeks), Author's Approach:

Chapter 1: Who Cares about Ethics?

Chapter 2: Stories with Morals

Chapter 3: Ethical Relativism

Chapter 4: Myself or Others?

Chapter 5: Using Your Reason Part 1: Utilitarianism

Chapter 6: Using Your Reason Part 2: Kant's Deontology

Chapter 7: Personhood, Rights, and Justice

Chapter 8: Socrates, Plato, and the Good Life

Chapter 9: Aristotle's Virtue Theory

Chapter 10: Modern Perspectives

Chapter 11: Different Gender, Different Ethic?

Chapter 12: Virtues, Values, and Religion

Chapter 13: Case Studies in Virtue

Chapter 14: Conclusion: The Moral Importance of Stories

One Semester (15–18 weeks), Alternative Approach with Focus on Virtue Ethics:

Chapter 1: Who Cares about Ethics?

Chapter 2: Stories with Morals

Chapter 8: Socrates, Plato, and the Good Life

Chapter 9: Aristotle's Virtue Theory

Chapter 10: Modern Perspectives

Chapter 11: Different Gender, Different Ethic?

Chapter 12: Virtues, Values, and Religion

Chapter 13: Case Studies in Virtue

Chapter 3: Ethical Relativism

Chapter 4: Myself or Others?

Chapter 5: Using Your Reason Part 1: Utilitarianism
Chapter 6: Using Your Reason Part 2: Kant's Deontology
Chapter 7: Personhood, Rights, and Justic
Chapter 14: Conclusion: The Moral Importance of Stories

One Quarter (10 weeks), Possible Approaches:

1. *Focus on classical conduct and virtue theories:*

   Chapter 1: Who Cares about Ethics?
   Chapter 2: Stories with Morals
   Chapter 3: Ethical Relativism
   Chapter 4: Myself or Others?
   Chapter 5: Using Your Reason Part 1: Utilitarianism
   Chapter 6: Using Your Reason Part 2: Kant's Deontology
   Chapter 7: Personhood, Rights, and Justice
   Chapter 8: Socrates, Plato, and the Good Life
   Chapter 9: Aristotle's VirtueTheory
   Chapter 13: Case Studies in Virtue
   Chapter 14: Conclusion: The Moral Importance of Stories

2. *Focus on Conduct and Virtue Theories with emphasis on a contemporary aspect*

   Chapter 1: Who Cares about Ethics?
   Chapter 2: Stories with Morals
   Chapter 3: Ethical Relativism
   Chapter 4: Myself or Others?
   Chapter 5: Using Your Reason Part 1: Utilitarianism
   Chapter 6: Using Your Reason Part 2: Kant's Deontology
   Chapter 7: Personhood, Rights, and Justice
   Chapter 10: Modern Perspectives
   Chapter 11: Different Gender, Different Ethic?
   Chapter 13: Case Studies in Virtue
   Chapter 14: Conclusion: The Moral Importance of Stories

3. *Focus on a Cross-Cultural Perspective*

   Chapter 1: Who Cares about Ethics?
   Chapter 2: Stories with Morals
   Chapter 3: Ethical Relativism
   Chapter 4: Myself or Others?
   Chapter 5: Using Your Reason Part 1: Utilitarianism
   Chapter 6: Using Your Reason Part 2: Kant's Deontology

Chapter 7: Personhood, Rights, and Justice
Chapter 8: Socrates, Plato, and the Good Life
Chapter 11: Different Gender, Different Ethic?
Chapter 12: Virtues, Values, and Religion
Chapter 13: Case Studies in Virtue
Chapter 14: Conclusion: The Moral Importance of Stories

4. *Focus on a historical approach* (such a selection is not part of the book's design, but it is an option to piece together a strictly historical approach).

Chapter 1: Who Cares about Ethics?
Chapter 2: Stories with Morals
Chapter 8: Socrates, Plato, and the Good Life
Chapter 9: Aristotle's Virtue Theory
Chapter 12: Virtues, Values, and Religion
Chapter 5: Using Your Reason Part 1: Utilitarianism
Chapter 6: Using Your Reason Part 2: Kant's Deontology
Chapter 7: Personhood, Rights, and Justice
Chapter 10: Modern Perspectives
Chapter 11: Different Gender, Different Ethic?
Chapter 13: Case Studies in Virtue
Chapter 14: Conclusion: The Moral Importance of Stories

CLASS PRESENTATION MATERIALS:
A DETAILED OVERVIEW

Part 1: The Story As a Tool of Ethics

Part 1 defines the concepts of ethics, morals, and values, and introduces the narrative as one medium through which morals may be taught and discussed.

Chapter 1: Who Cares about Ethics?

This introductory chapter outlines the growing interest in moral issues. The terminology of ethics, morals, and values is introduced and discussed, and the discussion then focuses on different groups in society showing an interest in ethical issues (such as organized religion, the media, the medical world, the scientific world, and the entertainment industry). The concept of Narratives used as teaching tools in ethics is introduced and illustrated with two examples: the films *Jurassic Park* and *Working Girl*.

Main Points

Ethics, Morals, and Values

- The difference between ethics and morals: *Morality* refers to moral rules we follow, while *ethics* refers to theories about these rules: questioning and justifying the rules.

AUTHOR'S TIP

You may want to ask your students whether they would have different expectations of the course if it were titled "Introduction to morals" or "Introduction to Ethics" or "Introduction to Values." Most students will, instinctively, perceive of a "morals" course as being somehow restrictive.

- The concept of values: Only philosophy can evaluate whether people's values are justified.
- Should schools teach values? Since we live in a multicultural society it is better for schools to focus on ethics, rather than on specific moral rules.

Who Thinks Ethics Is Important?

- Philosophy: Ethics is one of the major branches of philosophical inquiry.

- Organized religion: Religion has a special interest in the moral standards of the congregation. For many people ethics and religion are inseparable, but it is possible to have secular ethical standards.

- Medicine: The accomplishments of medical research make it necessary to develop a new kind of ethical responsibility. Example: The issue of human cloning.

- Science: Scientific research needs to be aware of an ethical dimension: Just because something is possible, does it mean science has to do it? Example: The Tuskegee Syphilis Study.

- Business: The business world is becoming increasingly aware of ethical requirements and standards.

- The Law: Morals and laws do not always coincide, although the law usually follows public opinion. Introduction of two traditional aspects of legal philosophy: Naturalism and legal positivism.

- Journalism: Journalists must be aware of the ethics of reporting a news story.

- The Entertainment Industry: The preoccupation with moral issues in the entertainment industry often focuses on sex. The need for responsibility of the entertainment industry, especially in telling stories of violence. Recent responses to criticism in Hollywood.

- Online Services and the Internet: The issue of free speech on the Internet is raised.

Why Have Rules of Moral Conduct?

- The basic questions: Is morality a matter of the heart, or does it come from reason? Is morality a biological fail-safe, and are we all egoists at heart? How should one solve moral dilemmas? Reference to Part 2 and its main question, *What should I do?*

Ethics in Narratives

- The plot-outlines in *The Moral of the Story* have two purposes: (1) to supply a foundation for discussion, and (2) to inspire the students to experience the stories in their original form.

- A brief introduction to the increasing use of stories as tools to teach and learn moral lessons is illustrated by four examples: Bibliotherapy, the Orion Society policy, medical training, and cross-cultural understanding.

Science and Ethics

- Frankenstein's monster is the prototype of all stories where science has disregarded moral values.

Narrative

- *Jurassic Park*, film (1993). Summary. A businessman recreates dinosaurs genetically with the help of scientists in the hope of opening a theme park. A paleoanthropologist and a paleobotanist become involved and are in danger when the dinosaurs get loose. A summary of the popular film is used to discuss the question, Just because it is possible for science to do something, does it mean science ought to do it?

SOME ADDITIONAL NARRATIVES ILLUSTRATING
THE THEME OF SCIENCE AND ETHICS*

The theme of the "mad scientist," or research without a conscience for the sake of knowledge or profit, is covered in numerous works of literature and films. Some suggestions are:

Dr. Jekyll and Mr. Hyde (1886) short story, made into films a number of times, many of them with a new twist to the story.

The Fly, film (1956, remade 1986)

The China Syndrome, film (1979)

Wild Palms, television miniseries (1993)

Mary B. Shelley, *Frankenstein*, or *The Modern Prometheus*, novel (1818)

All the Frankenstein films

Dr. Strangelove, film (1964)

The Island of Dr. Moreau, film (1977, remade 1996)

Business Ethics

Narrative

- *Working Girl* (1998). Summary. The issue of business ethics is illustrated by a plot summary. A young secretary's idea is stolen by her boss, and the secretary embarks on an impersonation scheme, playing a business executive in the hope that her idea may be accepted. The summary is used to discuss the various breaches of business ethics happening in the film.

SOME ADDITIONAL NARRATIVES ILLUSTRATING
THE THEME OF BUSINESS ETHICS

Henrik Ibsen, *A Doll's House*, play (1979). See Chapter 11 for a summary and excerpt.

Bertholt Brecht, *Threepenny Opera*, play (1928)

Arthur Miller, *Death of a Salesman*, play (1948). Made into a film 1951 and 1985.

Save the Tiger, film (1973)

---

* Throughout this manual you will find a selection of suggestions for additional stories to discuss. Titles may appear several times, as they can be used to illustrate several different moral problems. In these selections of additional stories I have chosen primarily "mainstream" stories, usually available through bookstores and/or video rental outlets. The order of the titles is chronological.

Wall Street, film (1987)

Glengarry Glen Ross, film (1992)

The Firm, film (1993)

Barbarians at the Gate, film (1993)

Disclosure, film (1994)

AUTHOR'S TIP

There is a whole category of fiction exploring the professional ethics of the characters in the story, all the way from ethics among architects, doctors, and lawyers, to "honor among thieves." If the students are receptive, you may want to explore this theme further. A few examples are: *The Fountainhead* (novel and film), R*io Bravo* (film), *The Professionals* (film), *The Godfather* (film), *A Few Good Men* (film, see Chapter 10 for summary) , and *Carlito's Way* (film).

Boxes

1.1   *Moral and Nonmoral Values* Introduces the concepts of moral and nonmoral oughts, with examples.

1.2   *Family Values* Discusses the concept of family values from a conservative and a liberal view.

1.3   *Value-free Science?* Discusses the connection between scientific research and private interests, based on Jürgen Habermas's critique.

Chapter 2: Stories with Morals

This chapter introduces the idea that we often learn moral lessons from the stories we are exposed to at an early age as well as later in life. With numerous examples from world literature and film this chapter explores the relationship between fact and fiction and looks at the way stories have been told in order to teach moral lessons, from ancient myths to novels, short stories, and films. We examine different genres of stories as they affect our moral outlook (such as Westerns, science fiction, and war stories). The power of the story serving as a role model for behavior is discussed and related to the classical discussions by Plato and Aristotle about the value of drama, and the modern therapeutic phenomenon of telling one's own story is explored. The chapter concludes with primary readings from Plato and Aristotle, and the following narratives: Euripides' *The Bacchants* and Quentin Tarantino's *Pulp Fiction.*

Main Points

Learning Moral Lessons from Stories

Main Points

Learning Moral Lessons from Stories

The Storytellers

- The cultural tradition of telling stories in order to teach the new generation about moral values. This tradition survives in modern novels and films.

Never Cry Wolf! and Other Didactic Stories

- Powerful stories help children learn moral lessons, such as "The Boy Who Cried Wolf."

- Other examples of stories with a message: "Little Fir Tree" and *Peter Pan.*

- Stories are increasingly recognized as moral tools by philosophers.

- Stories that moralize—didactic stories—are contrasted with stories that tell an open-ended tale of moral problems.

AUTHOR'S TIP

You may want to tell your students the following bit of news from the Italian town of L'Aquila, June 1996: A judge sentenced a seventeen-year old boy who had stolen valuable antiquarian books to reading four novels over a period of six months. After six months the boy would have to prove to the judge that he had read and understood the books. The first two books assigned were Italian classics, and the last two were left to the boy to choose. If he succeeded in persuading the judge that he had indeed read the books, the judge would drop the charge of theft. Your students may want to discuss the meaning of this sentence, and whether it might serve the purpose intended!

Telling Stories

Fact, Fiction, or Both?

- Even factual stories are enriched with poetic creativity.

Stories with a Moral Lesson

- Myths: Storytelling of the Beginning time of the culture, serving as moral explanations and roles to emulate.

- Fairy tales: Entertainment with an edge of wishful thinking.

- Parables: Religious allegories about the moral demands of God. Example: "The Prodigal Son."

- A story of sacrifice: The story of Abraham and Isaac, as it has been subjected to several interpretations, including that of Søren Kierkegaard. (The subject of the sacrifice of Isaac is resumed in Chapter 10).

- Fables and counter-fables: Moralizing (didactic) stories primarily for children. Stories by Hans Christian Andersen and Mark Twain as examples of antimoralizing narratives.

Stories as Role Models

Who Are Our Heroes?

- Our heroes are not always good people; we also learn lessons from "bad" people who mend their ways, or "bad" people who are rightfully punished.

Some Contemporary Moral Lessons

- Moral lessons taught in older stories may not always have the same effect. Example: *Brave New World.*

- The following genres represent story types that often incorporate moral problems.

  Wartime ethics: Although war is no longer glorified, we may still enjoy hearing stories of the courage and loyalty of the soldier.

  The moral universe of Westerns: The moral potential of the Western has been utilized over the decades for different ideological purposes.

  Science fiction: This genre explores moral problems in connection with topics such as genetic manipulation, environmental disasters, and artificial intelligence.

Crime and suspense: The changing nature of crime-fighting stories shows a shift in interest from simple who-dunnits to tales of corruption among police officers.

Stories to Live and Die By

- Novels are capable of affecting the reader greatly. Example: Goethe's *The Sorrows of Werther.*

AUTHOR'S TIP

It is not unlikely that some of your students have been affected by a friend's or a relative's suicide or suicide attempt. In connection with *Werther* it may be appropriate to get the subject out in the open and talk about copycat suicides among teens, or teen suicides inspired by the actions of music idols such as Kurt Cobain. The issue of suicide will be brought up again in Chapter 5 in connection with John Stuart Mill's harm principle.

- Exploring the issue of violence in movies and on TV, including the copy-cat phenomenon from recent years, and drawing a parallel to the debate in ancient Greece: Contrasting Plato's and Aristotle's views on the effects of drama: For Plato, drama is harmful because it undermines the mental balance of the audience. For Aristotle, drama can be emotionally cathartic; however, Aristotle would also recommend moderation in how many dramas you watch.

- Often the stories that affect us the most are those in which the hero has a flawed character, and the question often becomes whether such a person's life is somehow redeemed through the story.

Stories to Change the World

- Stories involving social criticism often have great effect on the world of readers, such as *Gulliver's Travels, 1984,* and *The Trial.*

Seeing Life as a Story

Living in Time

- The temporal structure of the mind: Remembering the past and anticipating the future.

- With temporal experience comes awareness of mortality.

Telling Your Own Story

- Three key features to telling one's own story: The story is selective, incomplete, and to some extent, fictional.

15

- However, it can be a useful tool to get a grip on one's identity, including one's role as a member of one's community and culture.

When Bad Things Happen

- Erikson's concept of ego integrity; the challenge to ego integrity when something unexpected and bad happens.

- Ways of dealing with such an occurrence: (1) to see it as the hand of God, or fate; (2) to interpret it as karma from past lives; (3) to see it as the sufferer's own fault.

Searching for a Meaning

- An alternate way (4): stories help us deal emotionally with the unexpected.

- The stories of traditional cultures may teach a different lesson than stories in modern cultures.

- The identity crisis arises when life doesn't make sense anymore, due to bad and unforeseen events.

- The help of narratives: We can rewrite our own story and find a new meaning by reinterpreting past events and seeing them in a new pattern, a new "plot."

- This is not only a redescription, it is also a moral prescription for the future.

Primary Readings

- Plato, *The Republic,* excerpt from Book X: Socrates proves to Glaucon that it is harder to maintain one's emotional equilibrium if one witnesses a person in a drama whose emotions are out of control.

- Aristotle, *Poetics.* Excerpts from Chapters 6, 13, and 14: Aristotle demonstrates what makes a good dramatic plot—that an ordinary person experiences a fall from happiness to misery because of an error in judgment. In addition, Aristotle argues that drama can have a cathartic effect on our emotions.

Narratives

- Euripides, *The Bacchants*, play (5th century B.C.E.), excerpt. A stranger has come to town, professing the power of the new religion of Dionysus. The young king, Pentheus, is skeptical, even though his mother Agave, the king's daughter, is actively engaged in the Dionysus-cult. The stranger, whose true identity is Dionysus himself, tricks Pentheus into spying on his mother during the secret orgiastic rites, with the result that his mother kills him, believing that she is killing a mountain lion. The excerpt from the play is used to discuss the value of violent dramatic art.

- *Pulp Fiction*, film (1994), summary of one scene. The hit men Vincent and Jules are retrieving a briefcase for their boss, and in the process they kill several kill several young men guarding the briefcase. Their own contact is killed by accident, his death making a mess in their car. After a hasty but thorough clean-up they have breakfast in a diner that happens to be hit by a young couple demanding money. The summary is used to discuss violence used as an anti-violence message; in addition, the issue of profanity is raised.

AUTHOR'S TIP

Pulp Fiction has inspired many viewers to speculate about unexplained details in the film. The briefcase, for instance: What does it contain? What is it that emits such a mysterious glow? *Pulp Fiction* fans on the Internet suggest the following solution, supposedly quoted from "a friend of a friend of Tarantino's," and you may want to share this with your students: The content of the briefcase is no less than the soul of the gangster Wallace, being reclaimed from the devil by Jules and Vincent. The band-aid on the back of Wallace's neck supposedly hints at the deal with the devil who, according to legend, removes the soul from just that spot. And since the two hit men are actually fighting the devil, the incident of the bullets that missed is, indeed, divine intervention! Another hint of the supernatural connection is the combination on the briefcase: 666. According to Tarantino himself the question is open: The briefcase contains anything you want it to contain.

SOME ADDITIONAL NARRATIVES ILLUSTRATING THE ISSUE OF VIOLENCE

Aeschylus, *Agamemnon*, play (5th century B.C.E.)

Sheri S. Tepper, *Grass*, novel (1989)

Reservoir Dogs, film (1992)

Once Were Warriors, film (1994)

Natural Born Killers, film (1994)

Clockers, film (1995)

Boxes

2.1 *Kafka's Abraham* Discusses Franz Kafka's version of the Abraham legend.

2.2 *Some War Movies with a Message* Looks at war movies that try to remain as factual as possible, and war movies that provide a looser historical interpretation.

2.3 *The Changing Messages of Westerns* Westerns have the capability of exploring current issues; the changing issues in traditional and recent Westerns.

2.4 *Socrates, Plato, and Aristotle* A brief introduction to the three Greek thinkers.

17

2.5 *Do Slasher Movies Teach a Lesson?* The hidden messages of slasher movies: Life is cheap, and sex and death are somehow connected.

2.6 *The Non-Human Who Wants to Become Human* The moral situation of the artificial human being who helps us identify what humanity is.

2.7 *The Good Guys and the Bad Guys* The moral confusion in suspense-stories: Cops as good and bad guys.

2.8 *Fictional Friends* Some examples of characters in books and films that have come to feel like personal friends to many.

Part 2: What Should I Do? Theories of Conduct

Part 2 examines the most influential theories of ethical conduct in Western philosophy.

Chapter 3: Ethical Relativism

This chapter explains the theory of ethical relativism. As an introductory issue the question of moral differences is discussed, leading up to the lesson taught by anthropology that morality is a matter of acculturation. The view of relativity is questioned and contrasted to the approach of soft universalism. Finally, a discussion of cultural diversity outlines the pros and cons of ethical relativism.

Main Points

How to Deal with Moral Differences

- Four major ways to approach moral differences: (1) moral nihilism and skepticism, (2) ethical relativism, (3) soft universalism, and (4) hard universalism (absolutism).

The Lessons of Anthropology

- A presentation of the theories of cultural and ethical relativism, and an analysis of how they differ.
- King Darius compares Greek and Callatian funeral practices.
- According to the anthropologist Ruth Benedict, the concept of the normal is a variant of the concept of the good.
- Discussion of Benedict's example of the Northwest Coast Indians.

Is Tolerance All We Need?

- The Singapore caning incident.

Problems with Ethical Relativism

- There are circumstances where the tolerance of ethical relativism seems inappropriate, such as in cases of nations committing genocide on their own population, and nations allowing infanticide and female circumcision.

  (1) Relativism precludes learning from other cultures.

  (2) Relativism acknowledges only majority rule.

  (3) Are we talking about the professed or the actual morality of a culture?

AUTHOR'S TIP

As part of the discussion of the problem of professed or actual morality you may want to ask your students to come up with examples of a majority population officially supporting one moral viewpoint and unofficially following another standard—the phenomenon we usually call a "double standard." Possible examples of such behavior may be sexual morals in different time periods (such as the Victorian era) and the ideal of honesty.

---

  (4) There is a practical problem deciding what a majority is.

  (5) Tolerance can't be a universal value according to the logic of ethical relativism.

Refuting Ethical Relativism

The Flat Earth Argument

- The mere fact that there is cultural disagreement doesn't ascertain that no common ground can be found.

The Problem of Induction

- The problem of induction (the fact that no absolute answer can be reached through empirical research) precludes relativism's rejection of a common moral ground.

Soft Universalism

- All cultures have at least some values in common, even if they express them in different ways.

- James Rachels's three universal values: Caring for enough infants to keep society going; prohibition of lying; prohibition of murder.

- Descriptive and normative soft universalism.

The New Relativism of Cultural Diversity

- Monoculturalism and multiculturalism; the "melting pot" and the "tossed salad."

- Exclusive multiculturalism (particularism) vs. inclusive multiculturalism (pluralism).

- Problem with inclusive multiculturalism: An overwhelming curriculum.

- Problem with exclusive multiculturalism: May lead to a new form of segregation. May be hard to administer in a culture of mixed racial and ethnic ancestry.

- Inclusive multiculturalism can work as a form of soft universalism.

AUTHOR'S TIP

Many students have personal experiences with cultural diversity. You may want to ask for student contributions in the form of presentations or papers, asking their opinion on exclusive vs. inclusive multiculturalism. You should expect a variety of presentations, some very personal and not necessarily of clearly defined philosophical content; however, a certain amount of leeway will probably be useful in order for students to be assured that their contribution and viewpoint are relevant, or at least can be shaped into a relevant philosophical argument. On occasion the classroom experience can become rather polarized during such presentations; not all students relate well to being exposed to the "differentness" of others nor feel comfortable talking about their own experience, but I have found that the majority of students are genuinely open-minded and interested. However, I also find that most students prefer to just be "members of the student community" rather than emphasize their own ethnicity in front of the class.

Primary Readings

- Ruth Benedict, "Anthropology and the Abnormal" (1934), excerpt. In this excerpt Benedict tells of the Melanesian paranoid society where it is good manners to assume that there is danger of being poisoned.

- Bhikhu Parekh, "The Concept of Multicultural Education" (1986), excerpt. Parekh outlines the ill effects of a monocultural education for the minority child as well as for the child from the dominant culture.

Narratives

- Alice Walker, *Possessing the Secret of Joy*, novel (1993), excerpt. In this excerpt we meet Tashi, who is in prison awaiting her trial for murder. She has killed M'Lissa of the Olinka tribe where she has lived for much of her adult life, because the shaman woman is responsible for the genital mutilation (female circumcision) of the young girls in the tribe, including Tashi herself.

We also meet her American husband, Adam, who tries to understand what his wife has gone through, and we see the situation from the point of view of the shaman herself. The excerpt is used as a criticism of the tolerance of ethical relativism: Must we stand by and watch people's lives, health, and happiness be jeopardized in the name of cultural diversity?

- E. M. Forster, *A Passage to India*, novel (1924) and film (1984), summary. *A Passage to India* tells about the misunderstandings between a young British woman and an Indian doctor in early twentieth century India. The cultural clash of different expectations and prejudice is only barely resolved in the narrative. The summary is used to discuss the merits of ethical relativism and soft universalism.

- Spike Lee, *Do The Right Thing*, film (1989), summary. *Do The Right Thing* illustrates the issue of racial and cultural diversity in a Brooklyn neighborhood. In a predominantly black neighborhood, an Italian pizza restaurant is the focus of attention, and later of violence. A young black man is killed by the police, and a riot ensues. The story is used to discuss the concept of multiculturalism.

SOME ADDITIONAL NARRATIVES ILLUSTRATING THE THEME OF CULTURAL DIVERSITY AND ETHICAL RELATIVISM

William Shakespeare, *The Merchant of Venice*, play (1600)

Ralph Ellison, *Invisible Man*, novel (1947)

Doris Lessing, *The Grass is Singing*, novel (1950)

Hester Street, film (1975)

M. M. Kaye, *The Far Pavillions*, novel (1978). (Has been made into a fairly good television miniseries, but I suggest not using the two-hour video version. It is too abbreviated to make any points whatsoever.)

Moscow on the Hudson, film (1984).

My Beautiful Laundrette, film (1985)

Jungle Fever, film (1990)

A Stranger Among Us, film (1992).

Sheri S. Tepper, *Sideshow*, novel (1992).

Thunderheart, film (1992)

Mississippi Masala, film (1992)

Michael Crichton, *Rising Sun*, novel and film (1993)

My Family/Mi Familia, film (1995)

The Perez Family, film (1995)

Lawrence of Arabia, film, (1962)

The Last of the Mohicans, film (1992)

Bopha!, film (1993)

Heaven and Earth, film (1993)

Amy Tan, *The Joy Luck Club,* novel (1989), film (1993)

Bread and Chocolate, film (1976)

Boxes

3.1 *Descriptive and Normative Ethics* Analyzes the difference between descriptive and normative ethics, and introduces the concept of metaethics.

3.2 *The Psychology of Becoming a Moral and Social Being* Compares Benedict's concept of moral socialization with Freud's concept of the Superego.

3.3 *How to Test a Theory* Introduces the philosophical procedure of testing a theory to find its breaking point.

3.4 *Cultural Diversity or Cultural Adversity?* The danger of assuming that the viewpoint of a group is wrong or right just by virtue of being held by the group: an *Ad hominem* argument.

Chapter 4: Myself or Others?

Here we move to the classical question of egoism. First, the theory of psychological egoism is defined and discussed. Secondly, ethical egoism is presented and discussed, and the concept of consequentialism is introduced. Finally, the alternative of altruism is discussed.

Main Points

Psychological Egoism

Definition of the Theory

- A psychological, descriptive theory claiming that people behave selfishly.

AUTHOR'S TIP

While most philosophers take "ought implies can" to mean that something can't be a duty if a person is unable to perform it, there is another possible meaning, explored by Johann Gottlieb Fichte: "If I ought, I can." In other words, "where there is a will, there is a way." Your students may enjoy discussing the difference between the two interpretations, and in particular whether there is any merit to Fichte's version.

All People Look After Themselves

- Plato's story of the Ring of Gyges

- Three reasons why psychological egoism is popular: (1) appeal to honesty, (2) revisionist cynicism, and (3) an easy way to avoid considering the interests of others.

Shortcomings of Psychological Egoism

(1) Falsification is not possible (the principle of falsification).

(2) Is doing what we want always selfish? Abraham Lincoln rescues the pigs from the mud.

(3) Problems of language: Inventing words; the fallacy of the suppressed correlative.

- The bottom line criticism of psychological egoism: Either it is not true (not everyone is selfish to the bone) or it is uninteresting (everyone is a little bit selfish).

AUTHOR'S TIP

Ask your students for contributions in the form of examples of altruistic deeds, and then proceed to dismiss them on the basis of psychological egoism. This is likely to convert your students to psychological egoism in a very short time, but here you may want to point out that this ability of psychological egoism to always get the last word is no advantage for a theory (the principle of falsification). Psychological egoism can probably only be defeated when criticized for its foundational assumptions, not through empirical examples.

Ethical Egoism

Definition of the Theory

- A normative theory about how we ought to behave: Selfishly.

You Should Look After Yourself

- A version of the Golden Rule, with emphasis on oneself.

- Ethical egoism is a consequentialist theory.

Shortcomings of Ethical Egoism

- Socrates' answer to Glaucon: A selfish person can't be happy.

- The argument that ethical egoism is self-contradictory.

23

- The argument that ethical egoism only works if you advocate altruism while you yourself pursue egoism, but this can't be universalized.

Altruism: Ideal and Reciprocal

> **AUTHOR'S TIP**
>
> In the discussion of animals and altruism, you may want to remind your students of Binti, the gorilla female who in 1996 rescued a small boy who had fallen into the zoo gorilla enclosure. She carried him over to the door where she knew the keeper would appear, and protected him from harm. Binti had been raised in a family of humans, but had not been trained for situations of rescue. Animal behaviorists who work with the great apes have expressed little surprise; many claim that one might expect this caring behavior from some individuals, just as one might expect other individuals to show uncaring behavior (as one researcher remarked: not unlike humans).

- Cases of humans and animals sacrificing themselves for the good of others.
- Golden Rule Altruism
- Peter Singer's version of the Prisoner's Dilemma.
- Tentative evidence of rules of behavior among chimpanzees.

> **AUTHOR'S TIP**
>
> Your students may wonder about the classical formulation of the Prisoner's Dilemma, and here you'll find a brief summary of it (summarized from James Rachels, the second edition of *The Elements of Moral Reasoning*). You and Smith are both political prisoners of a totalitarian regime, and you are each told that the length of your sentence will depend on whether you confess or not. If you confess and Smith doesn't, you will be sentenced to one year in prison and Smith will get ten years. If neither confesses, each will get two years. If both confess, each will get five years. If Smith confesses and you don't, you will get ten. If your only goal is to limit your sentence, logic demands that you should confess, because you will be ahead whether or not Smith also confesses. However, since Smith is thinking along the same lines, chances are that, while looking out for your own interests, you will both confess and both get five years. However, if you think of Smith's interests also, and can be fairly certain that he (or she) is thinking of yours, then it will be to your mutual advantage: If you both don't confess, both will get out after only two years.

Primary Reading

- Ayn Rand, "The Ethics of Emergencies" (1963), excerpt. Here Rand criticizes the concept of altruism as she sees it, and redefines the term of sacrifice.

24

Narratives

- *Hero*, film (1992), summary. *Hero* is the story of a small-time thief who saves all crew and passengers of a downed airliner, only to see another man take credit for it. The narrative is used to discuss the nature of selfishness and unselfishness.

- *Madame Bovary,* novel (1857), films (1949 and 1991), summary and excerpt. This is the story of a young woman who is bored in her provincial life, and selfishly sets out to entertain herself. The story is used to discuss selfishness and self-interest.

- *Atlas Shrugged,* novel (1957), excerpt. This section of the mammoth novel illustrates ethical egoism in Ayn Rand's version: Letting yourself be abused by parasites is morally wrong. The steelworks owner Rearden is confronted by a railroad tycoon, forcing him to reevaluate his principles.

SOME ADDITIONAL NARRATIVES ILLUSTRATING THE THEME OF EGOISM

Honoré de Balzac, *Père Goriot*, novel (1834).

Rudyard Kipling, "The Man Who Would Be King," short story (1888–1890); made into an excellent film (1975). See it in letterbox.

Margaret Mitchell, *Gone with the Wind,* novel (1937), film (1939)

Nightmare Alley, film (1947)

Rashomon, film (1950)

The Blue Max, film (1966)

Save the Tiger, film (1973)

Wall Street, film (1987)

The Story of Women, film (1988)

Pretty Woman, film (1990)

Goodfellas, film (1990)

Money for Nothing, film (1993)

Isabel Allende, *The House of the Spirits*, novel (1985), film (1993)

Carolyn Chute, *Merry Men*, novel (1994)

Casino, film (1995)

SOME ADDITIONAL NARRATIVES ILLUSTRATING THE THEME OF ALTRUISM

"Faithful John," *Grimm's Fairy Tales*, short story (1812–1815)

Charles Dickens, *A Tale of Two Cities*, novel, (1859), film (1935, 1958)

Henrik Ibsen, *The Wild Duck,* play (1884)

Ernest Hemingway, *For Whom the Bell Tolls*, novel (1940), film (1943)

Casablanca, film (1942)

This Land Is Mine, film (1943)

Titanic, film (1953). May also be used to illustrate egoism!

The Alamo, film (1961). Use letterbox Director's Cut from 1992, restoring important missing scenes.

The Sacrifice, film, 1986

Glory, film (1989)

The Abyss, film (1989). As an illustration of altruism, use only the Director's Cut from 1993; in the 1989 version important sequences have been cut.

Alive, film (1993)

Godfather Mendoza, film (1933)

The Bicycle Thief, film (1948)

The Official Story, film (1986)

Germinal, film (1994)

Il Postino/The Postman, film (1995)

The Age of Innocence, film (1993)

Boxes

4.1   *Egoism or Egotism?* Identifies the differences in meaning.

4.2   *Selfish vs. Self-interested* Discusses the implications of using these terms to identify psychological egoism.

4.3   *Ought Implies Can* Analyzes the meaning of the idea that we are not obliged to do something it is impossible for us to do.

4.4 *Hobbes and the Feeling of Pity* Discusses Thomas Hobbes's idea that all emotions are reflections of self-love, including pity.

4.5 *Hedonism* Introduces the concept of hedonism, and the paradox of hedonism: The harder you seek pleasure, the more it eludes you.

4.6 *Lincoln—Humble Man, or Clever Jokester?* Examines the possible reasons behind Lincoln's statement that he saved the pigs for selfish reasons.

4.7 *Individual Ethical Egoism* Discusses and discards individual ethical egoism because it can't be universalized. Introduces universalizability.

4.8 *Psychological and Ethical Altruism* Discusses the possibility of psychological altruism.

4.9 *David Hume: Humans are Benevolent by Nature* Presents David Hume's theory of natural compassion.

Chapter 5, Using Your Reason, Part 1: Utilitarianism

Here utilitarianism is introduced as an alternative consequentialist theory through Bentham's concept of the hedonistic (hedonic) calculus. The advantages and disadvantages of the universe of utilitarianism are explored, and J. S. Mill's redefinition of utilitarianism in terms of higher and lower pleasures is discussed. Furthermore, Mill's harm principle is introduced, and the development from act to rule utilitarianism is briefly discussed.

Main Points

- Definition of the principle of utility.
- Comparison with other, nonutilitarian consequentialist theories.

Jeremy Bentham and the Hedonistic Calculus

Reforming the System of Justice

- The Age of Enlightenment and the general historical background for Bentham's project.
- The theory that happiness is intrinsically valuable.

The Hedonistic Calculus

- Bentham's seven steps in the hedonistic calculus.
- The calculus is used today in professional contexts.
- Criticism of Bentham's calculus: The values are arbitrary and biased.

The Uncertain Future

- It is difficult to make a utilitarian choice when you don't know the exact outcome of your intended action.

- J. S. Mill's answer to criticism of utilitarianism.

The Moral Universe of Utilitarianism: Advantages and Problems of Sheer Numbers

- The capacity for suffering makes one a member of the moral universe.

- What creates happiness or decreases unhappiness for the majority is morally right by definition.

- Moral problems in utilitarianism: Can a minority be sacrificed for the sake of the majority? And if so, under what circumstances?

John Stuart Mill: Higher and Lower Pleasures

Some Pleasures are Higher than Others

- J. S. Mill's background, personal crisis, and resolve to redesign utilitarianism.

- The distinction between higher and lower pleasures, and the test for identification of the higher pleasures.

- Mill's intellectual and personal relationship with Harriet Taylor.

easier ones. Also, I decided to include information about the relationship between Mill and Taylor in this edition because my own students have expressed a consistent interest in the subject year after year. If your students display an interest in Mill's personal life, you may want to suggest that they discuss his theory of higher pleasures in the light of his and Harriet Taylor's situation and ask whether Mill's personal life is or is not relevant for our understanding of his theory.

- Criticism of Mill's test: It is biased in favor of intellectual pleasures.

Mill's Political Vision: Equality, and No Harm To Others

- In defense of Mill: his wish to educate the general population in order to make more options available to everybody.

- The harm principle: the only legitimate reason for interference with people is if they do harm to others.

- Does the harm principle contradict the principle of higher pleasures?

AUTHOR'S TIP

The harm principle may provide for a good discussion, since it is a more liberal principle than the one the legislation of the United States is based on: Would the students approve of a principle that doesn't allow interference if a person does no harm to others, but only to him or herself? You may want to include in the discussion the concept of indirectly influencing/indirectly harming another person.

- Limitations to the harm principle, including Mill's leaning toward cultural paternalism.

Act and Rule Utilitarianism

- The classical principle of utility versus the formulation of rule utilitarianism.

- Evaluation of rule utilitarianism.

Primary Readings

- Jeremy Bentham, *An Introduction to the Principles of Morals and Legislation* (1789), excerpt. In this section Bentham identifies the principle of utility.

- John Stuart Mill, *Utilitarianism* (1863), excerpt. In this excerpt, Mill expresses his view of higher and lower pleasures and subsequently (in a section that is quoted less often) tells his view of what makes life enjoyable.

AUTHOR'S TIP

Because of requests from instructors who like to spend an extra amount of time on the issues of utilitarianism and deontology and who would like to use several Narratives as illustrations, both Chapter 5 and Chapter 6 have four Narratives each. Since the moral viewpoint in each story is either a support for or a criticism of utilitaranism of deontology, the Narratives in both chapters can generally be used to illustrate both theories.

- Johann Herman Wessel, "The Blacksmith and the Baker," satirical poem (1777), summary. Utilitarianism is criticized for its lack of concern for human rights in this story; a blacksmith is convicted of murder, but since the town can't afford to lose its blacksmith, they execute one of their two bakers instead.

- Fyodor Dostoyevsky, *The Brothers Karamazov*, novel (1881), excerpt. The two brothers Ivan and Alyosha are having a conversation about suffering and forgiveness. Ivan tells about an incident where a small boy was killed by a general for throwing a stone at the dogs. Ivan raises the question, Could one agree to a community's happiness being based on the suffering of a child? The excerpt is used to discuss the "sheer numbers" problem in utilitarianism: Can the end (a happy community) justify the means (a suffering few?)

- Ursula LeGuin, "The Ones Who Walk Away from Omelas," short story (1973), summary and excerpt. This story elaborates on the Dostoyevsky theme and tells of just such a community whose happiness is bought at the price of a child's suffering. (In the Dostoyevsky original there is also a section with a child being locked in a dark room, begging for forgiveness for she knows not what). Both stories criticizes the basic value of utilitarianism.

- *Outbreak*, film (1995), summary. This narrative is a medical drama where a scientist struggles to find a cure for an Ebola-like virus, and at the same time seeks to expose the politically motivated secrecy of his superiors. The story is used to discuss the principle of happiness: Is the well-being of the majority worth the sacrifice of a minority?

SOME ADDITIONAL NARRATIVES ILLUSTRATING
THE THEME OF UTILITARIANISM

Soylent Green, film (1973)

Rollerball, film (1975)

Star Trek: The Wrath of Khan, film (1982)

The Dead Zone, film (1983)

The Running Man, film (1987)

Orphan of Creation, novel (1988)

Indecent Proposal, film (1992)

Quiz Show, film (1994). Highly recommended as an alternative narrative to *Outbreak.* (I asked my students which one they would prefer to see in the new edition, and they all voted for *Outbreak*!)

Mulholland Falls, film (1996)

Boxes

5.1 *Intrinsic vs. Instrumental Value* Introduces the concept of value in itself and value leading to another value.

5.2 *What Is Happiness?* A brief discussion of what happiness means. Includes the anecdote about the prince looking for the shirt of a happy man.

5.3 *Who Can Suffer?* A brief overview of philosophical viewpoints from Descartes to contemporary theories of human and animal capacity for suffering.

5.4 *Mill and the Women's Cause* Mill's fight for equal rights, inspired by Harriet Taylor.

5.5 *The Naturalistic Fallacy* Discusses the problem inherent in Mill's argument that happiness is desirable because it is desired: moving from an "is" to an "ought."

Chapter 6: Using Your Reason, Part 2: Kant's Deontology

This chapter introduces Kant's deontology with the main focus on (1) the good will and the categorical imperative, and (2) the theory of rational beings as ends in themselves. The issue of absolutism (hard universalism) is discussed, as is the topic of autonomy.

Main Points

- Definition of deontology: Duty-theory.

To Do the Right Thing

The Good Will

What counts morally is not the assurance of good consequences, but the presence of a good will.

The Categorical Imperative

- Introduction to the categorical imperative, and to Immanuel Kant as a hard universalist.

- The example of the shopkeeper: Hypothetical vs. categorical imperative. Four options: (1) Cheat whenever feasible; (2) Don't cheat because I may be found out; (3) Don't cheat because I like my customers; (4) Don't cheat because it wouldn't be right.

- Kant's example of the man who wants to borrow money and who uses the categorical imperative to dissuade himself.

- Humans as autonomous lawmakers.

Kant's Critics

(1) J. S. Mill: Kant is referring to consequences.

(2) The categorical imperative can't solve a conflict between two duties.

(3) The categorical imperative allows for a loophole: describing a situation so specifically that it can't be universalized.

(4) The concept of "rational" may be ambiguous.

(5) The categorical imperative allows for no exceptions.

AUTHOR'S TIP

Here as in several other places in this edition I have opted for numbering the arguments, because I've found that it is easier for the students to remember them for test-taking purposes. In the test bank you will find corresponding questions.

Rational Beings Are Ends in Themselves

- Definition of means to an end versus end in oneself.

- The egalitarian aspect of Kant's principle.

- Rational beings are priceless value-givers, and should be treated with respect.

- One should not treat oneself as merely a means to an end, either.

- The difference between treating someone as a "means to an end," and as "merely a means to an end."

Beings Who Are Things

- The expansion of the moral universe to cover all rational beings.

- The problem with nonrational beings: Are animals and some categories of humans to be classified as "things"?

- Kant's later theory of the "right to a person akin to a thing": The gray area between person and thing.

- The kingdom of ends: The combination of the categorical imperative and the principle of not treating people as means may soften the hard universalist principle of the categorical imperative.

Primary Reading

- Immanuel Kant, *Metaphysics of Morals*, Book I, Chapter II, excerpt. This excerpt on lying (which provides wonderful discussion material) examines the various aspects of lying, including to oneself as well as to others, and evaluates the phenomenon of lying from both the categorical imperative and the rule of never treating oneself or others merely as a means to an end.

Narratives

- *Abandon Ship!,* film (1957), summary, is a real-life story about a shipwreck: The captain has to put passengers overboard the lifeboat in order to save the lives of the rest. Here utilitarianism is evoked as the only solution to a real life problem. *Abandon Ship!* can also be taken as an illustration of the universalization principle of the categorical imperative.

- *Rebel Without a Cause,* film (1955), summary, is a story about the generation gap; the son is in trouble, and needs advice and support from his father. The film contains a generational debate between utilitarianism and deontology: The father represents calculating utilitarianism, while the son represents the search for absolute rightness.

- *The Bridges of Madison County,* film (1995), summary. The film tells the story of a middle-aged Italian woman in a small Iowa farming community and her encounter with the love of her life, a traveling photographer. The moral issue of whether she should leave her husband and children for the sake of true love is used here to illustrate the categorical imperative: Would she want it to be a lesson for her daughter to learn about life and love?

- *Star Trek, The Next Generation*: "Justice." A young officer of Star Fleet faces execution for a minor offense on an absolutist planet. This episode criticizes an absolutist principle for not allowing for exceptions. It may also be used to illustrate another criticism of the categorical imperative: The conflict between duties. (The question of justice for Wesley is resumed in Box 7.3 in the following chapter. Also, Chapter 14 concludes with a parallel narrative, an episode from *Star Trek: Voyager* about another cultural clash between the crew of the *Voyager* and an alien race, devoted to the ideal of hedonism.)

SOME ADDITIONAL NARRATIVES ILLUSTRATING THE THEME OF DUTY AND OTHER KANTIAN THEMES

Honoré de Balzac, *Père Goriot,* novel (1834)

Henrik Ibsen, *Ghosts,* play (1881)

The Four Feathers, film (1939 [best version], 1977)

Mr. Smith Goes to Washington, film (1939)

Fort Apache, film (1948)

Twelve O'Clock High, film (1949)

Prince of Foxes, film (1951). Machiavellianism versus deontology.

High Noon, film (1952)

Shane, film (1952)

The Last Command, film (1955).

The Alamo, film (1961). Use letterbox Director's Cut from 1992, restoring important missing scenes.

The Conversation, film (1974)

Outland, film (1981)

The Last Starfighter, film (1984)

Gardens of Stone, film (1987)

Glory, film (1989)

The Remains of the Day, novel (1988) and film (1993)

The Age of Innocence, film (1993)

Six Degrees of Separation, film (1993). Good illustration of the phenomenon of lying.

The Simpsons, television series episode #1F05, 1993. A self-help guru admonishes Springfield to seek their "inner child" and follow Bart's maxim, "Do what you feel like." An entertaining illustration of the categorical imperative: If everyone follows Bart's maxim, then it will be undermined.

A Bronx Tale, film (1994)

Benny and Joon, film (1994). Can be used to raise questions about the nature of rationality.

Wyatt Earp, film (1994)

Priest, film (1994). Good illustration of conflict of duties.

Boxes

6.1   *Kant: His Life and Work* Introduces Immanuel Kant and his principal works.

6.2   *What Is Rationality?* A brief discussion of the controversial nature of the concept of rationality, also in terms of the gender issue and cultural diversity.

6.3   *Can Animals Think?* An overview of classical and recent theories about animal intelligence, including the results of research in animal language, with the example of Kanzi, the bonobo chimpanzee.

AUTHOR'S TIP

In the previous edition of this book the issues of animal suffering and intelligence were located in Chapter 14; that chapter is now gone from this edition. However, I find that the discussion of the effects of utilitarianism and Kantian deontology on the issue of ethics extended to nonhuman animals is too important to lose. For that reason I have incorporated the most pressing issues into Chapters 5, 6, and 7. In Chapter 5. Box 5.3 on animal

---

suffering provided a focal point for the extent of utilitarian concern. In this chapter Box 6.3 on animal intelligence allows the students to explore the idea of Kantian concern for rational beings. In Chapter 7 a section on rights includes the issue of animal rights.

Chapter 7: Personhood, Rights, and Justice

Personhood

- The Kantian question of what constitutes a person is still urgent.

What Is a Human Being?

- A discussion of physical criteria; the concept of personhood is not merely descriptive, but normative.

The Expansion of the Concept "Human"

- The development of the concept as a philosophical and political term.

Persons and Rights

- The development of the concept "person"; the issue of a person's rights and responsibilities is introduced.
- A discussion of rights and responsibilities applied to the historical situations of children, animals, and women.

The Question of Rights

Questions of Rights and Justice

- An introduction to the concept of natural rights.
- Bentham's and Mill's reactions to the idea of natural rights.

Dworkin: Rights Can't Be Traded for Benefits

- Dworkin's example of free speech as illustration of the issue: Should a basic right ever be outweighed by social benefits?
- Dworkin's two models: (1) We must seek a balance between the rights of the individual and the needs of society; (2) a basic right should not be abridged because of possible social harmful consequences. Dworkin agrees with model #2.

Rand and Hospers: Negative Rights

- Definition of negative rights: John Locke's concepts of rights to life, liberty, and property.

- Ayn Rand's description of the United States as a moral society, based on the right to one's own life.

- John Hospers defends the libertarian principle of negative rights.

- Consequences of a libertarian social policy.

Positive Rights

- The concept of positive rights to receive social goods is explained.

John Rawls: Justice as Fairness

- Modern liberalism identified as egalitarianism, and linked with positive as well as negative rights.

- Rawls's thought experiment: The original position; the veil of ignorance, as a means of reaching a fair distribution of social goods.

- An analogy: Cutting the birthday cake.

Reactions to Abstract Individualism: Wolgast and Friedman

- Wolgast outlines the Western history of individualism as ideology ("the atomistic model"), and criticizes it for being insufficient. Real life consists of other features not described by atomism such as human relationships and responsibilities.

- Wolgast here goes back to communitarianism, the political theory stating that a society is not merely a collection of individuals, but part of the purpose of the life of an individual. Rawls's theory is insufficient because it doesn't take our ties to our community into consideration.

- Friedman claims that the criticism of Rawls's abstract individualism often comes from feminists who see themselves as arms of a network rather than separate individuals.

- However, says Friedman, the danger of communitarianism is that it is often very traditional, and as such oppressive to women. We must be critical towards our own community traditions, too.

- In addition, communities are not a given; as adults we can choose our own communities, which need not even be live-in neighborhoods. So communitarianism must be more aware of changing communities and customs.

Rights, Duties, and Interests

- Kant's viewpoint of rights as linked with an understanding of duties precludes animal rights.

- Peter Singer and other philosophers instead link rights with interests; the expanding circle of morally significant beings.

AUTHOR'S TIP

Your students may have heard about the Great Ape Project, an international initiative started by Peter Singer and others, including scientists, for the purpose of securing rights for the great apes. If your students are interested, you may inform them that the Great Ape Project has an Internet website (at the time of writing this manual) where "Frequently Asked Questions" are answered. The Great Ape Project's goal is "to include the nonhuman great apes within the community of equals by granting them the basic moral and legal protection that only human beings currently enjoy." The Declaration on Great Apes demands the right to life, protection of individual liberty, and prohibition of torture of the great apes.

- According to Joel Feinberg, rights imply making moral claims against someone else, and in that case animals already have such rights, because they can be represented by humans in court.

- Steve Sapontzis argues that even if the range of interests of animals may be narrower than that of humans, humans don't have any right to disregard animal interests.

- The utilitarian approach to taking interests into consideration doesn't result in treating humans and nonhuman animals the same, but in taking their interests into equal consideration.

- Sapontzis chooses to expand Kantian ethics to cover animal intelligence; according to Kant all rational beings deserve respect, and for Sapontzis animals are now proven to be rational beings.

- Mary Ann Warren represents a less radical viewpoint with her idea that animals may be granted partial rights, only to be superseded by human interests in extreme cases.

Criminal Justice

- A distinction between distributive justice and criminal justice.

Five Common Approaches to Punishment

Forward-looking arguments, based on social utility:

1. Deterrence
2. Rehabilitation
3. Incapacitation

Backward-looking reasons, based on the guilt of the individual:

4. Retribution (lex talionis)
5. Vengeance, a non-legitimate but common reason.

Three major differences between retribution and vengeance:

1. Retribution is based on logic, while vengeance is emotional.
2. Retribution is a public act, while vengeance is private.
3. Retribution wants the punishment to fit the crime, while vengeance may be excessive.

The Issue of the Death Penalty

- Abolitionism is opposed to the death penalty, while retentionism is in favor of the death penalty.

- The five reasons for punishment and their relevance to the death penalty debate: Deterrence, incapacitation, retribution, and vengeance can all be used as retentionist arguments. Rehabilitation obviously cannot.

Primary Readings

- The United Nations Declaration of Human Rights, Articles 1 through 30.

- John Rawls, "Justice as Fairness" (1968), excerpt. In this excerpt Rawls discusses the two principles of justice: (1) Each person has an equal right to the most extensive liberty compatible with a like liberty for all, and (2) inequalities are arbitrary unless it is reasonable to expect that they will work out to everyone's advantage.

AUTHOR'S TIP

Since both the narratives are science fiction stories, it might be appropriate to remind the students of Chapter 2 where the capacity of science fiction for making social criticism is explored.

Narratives:

- *Blade Runner*, film (1982), summary. This story, now a cult classic, explores the lack of rights of intelligent artificial humans, replicants, in the near future. Created to perform dangerous jobs in the off-world colonies and then self-destruct, they come to earth seeking their inventor. The story is used to discuss the issue of personhood and rights.

- Larry Niven, "The Jigsaw Man" (1967), summary. In what some would call a prophetic story, Niven speculates that in the near future there will be a brisk illegal trade in organs for transplants, but the state will be involved in legal organ harvesting from executed criminals. Lew is awaiting his trial, knowing that he will be executed—for traffic violations. The story is used to discuss social utility as a reason for decisions involving justice and punishment.

AUTHOR'S TIP

While most students will probably dismiss the Niven scenario as outlandish, you may want to tell them that the trade in organs is brisk in many parts of the world (and the very idea of killing people for the value of their bodies is nothing new, as your students may remember from the caption to Bentham's picture in Chapter 5). Confirmed reports tell of people in third-world countries selling one of their own kidneys, as well as kidneys of their children, sometimes under the misapprehension that kidneys grow back. Rumors from South America tell of people, primarily children, disappearing and later turning up dead, with organs missing. As yet unconfirmed reports out of China tell of prisoners being executed in a manner that will accommodate organ transplants. The Niven scenario should be read as a caveat of social utility taken to an extreme, but it may certainly also be taken at face value: The organlegging scenario already seems a reality.

AUTHOR'S TIP

The study question #1 in "The Jigsaw Man" mentions a "slippery slope." You may want to spend some time explaining this phenomenon, a common form of the *reductio ad absurdum* argument, reducing one's opponent's viewpoint to absurdity. You may also want to stress that one doesn't have to "slide" all the way down the slope: It is possible to "draw the line." There are generally three ways to deal with slippery slope arguments: (1) One gives up one's original point of view (as in this case, that capital punishment should be linked with social utility); (2) one accepts the conclusion of the slope (such as, social utility justifies any means); and (3) one draws the line somewhere on the slope, and argues that there is a relevant difference between one point on the slope and the next (such as: Social utility may play a relevant part in the matter of punishment, provided that other factors are also decisive, such as matters of established guilt, and severity of crime).

SOME ADDITIONAL NARRATIVES ILLUSTRATING
THE THEMES OF PERSONHOOD, RIGHTS, AND JUSTICE

Personhood:

Pinocchio, film (1940)

Jorge Luis Borges, "The Circular Ruins," short story (1941)

Roger MacBride Allen, *Orphan of Creation,* novel (1988)

Star Trek, The Next Generation: "The Measure of a Man," television episode (1989)

Star Trek, The Next Generation: "The Offspring," television episode (1990)

Edward Scissorhands, film (1990)

Star Trek, The Next Generation: "The Quality of Life," television episode (1992). All three *Star Trek* episodes deal with the question of personhood by focusing on the android, Data, and other artificial life forms.

Rights and Justice:

Henrik Ibsen, *A Doll's House* (see Chapter 11)

Whose Life Is It, Anyway? film (1981)

Star Trek, The Next Generation: "Ethics," television episode (1992)

Bopha! film (1993)

In the Name of the Father, film (1993)

The Advocate, film (1994)

Dead Man Walking, film (1995)

Breaker Morant, film (1980)

Tom Wolfe, *Bonfire of the Vanities,* novel (1987)

Sophocles, *Antigone,* 5th century B.C.E.

Shakespeare, *Macbeth,* play (1606?), film (1848, 1971)

Heinrich von Kleist, *Michael Kohlhaus,* novel (1810)

Dickens, *A Tale of Two Cities,* novel (1859), film (1917, 1935, 1958, 1980)

Dostoyevsky, *Crime and Punishment,* novel (1866), film (1935 [two versions, French and U.S.] , 1958, 1959)

The Mark of Zorro, film (1920, 1940, 1974)

Kafka, *The Trial,* novel (1925), film (1963)

Walter Van Tilburg Clark, *The Oxbow Incident,* novel (1940), film (1943)

Bertolt Brecht, *The Caucasian Chalk Circle,* play (1944–45)

Twelve Angry Men, film (1957)

Good Day for a Hanging, film (1958)

Leonardo Sciascia, *Il Contesto,* novel (1971)

Nell, film (1994)

The Shawshank Redemption, film (1994)

Murder in the First, film (1995)

Dead Man Walking, film (1995)

Boxes

7.1   *Is the Fetus a Person?* A brief introduction to the pro-life (anti-choice) and pro-choice views of the abortion debate in terms of the concept of personhood. Mary Ann Warren's five criteria of personhood; Judith Jarvis Thomson's analogy of the violinist. Utilitarian and deontological approaches to the abortion issue.

7.2   *Bioethics: Humans Are not Commodities* The utilitarian approach to health care is characterized by the concept of quality of life. The QALY viewpoint is criticized by many who believe it represents a lack of respect for the life of those individuals with a low quality of life. Peter Kemp expresses the view that another person is irreplaceable and should never be sold out to the happiness of the majority.

7.3   *Star Trek: Justice for Wesley?* Referring to the Star Trek narrative in Chapter 6, the justice of the Kantian society is evaluated here in terms of the various theories of justice and punishment explored in this chapter.

Part 3: How Should I Be? Theories of Virtue

•   Part 3 examines the most influential theories of virtue in ancient and modern times.

Chapter 8: Socrates, Plato, and the Good Life

This chapter introduces the question of virtue ethics as an alternative or a supplement to theories of conduct, and discusses the concept of character. Next we look at Socrates' life and teachings and place him in a context of virtue ethics. Plato's role in ethics is examined, and his theory of forms is outlined.

Main Points

Virtue Ethics

What Is Virtue?

- Introduces virtue ethics, and the question of developing a good character (how should I be) vs. ethics of conduct (what should I do?).

AUTHOR'S TIP

The Greek word for "areté," or excellence, supposedly derives from Ares, the god of war. Furthermore, the Latin word-root for our word "Virtue" is *vir,* or male. You may want to ask your students to discuss these implications.

What Is Character?

- Discusses whether character is something you are born with and can't change, or whether character can be molded.

The Case for Virtue Ethics

- The decline of virtue ethics and the rise of ethics of conduct. Arguments in favor of a return to virtue ethics.

The Question of How to Live

The Good Teacher

- The teacher-student relationship between Socrates and Plato.
- Socrates: "The unexamined life is not worth living."

Socrates, Man of Athens

- The dialectic (Socratic) method.
- The life of Socrates as a man of the polis.

The Death of Socrates, the Works of Plato

- The trial and death of Socrates.
- Discussion about the background of the trial, and the issue of guilt or innocence.
- Plato's reaction; Plato's dialogues.

The Good Life

- The difference between opinion and true knowledge.

- Socrates' fight against relativism.

- Socrates' concept of virtue and truth-seeking.

The Virtuous Person

- The answer to Glaucon in the *Republic:* A virtuous person is in balance.

- The three parts of the psyche: Reason, spirit, and desires. Illustration: Plato's analogy of the charioteer.

- The political equivalent: The philosopher-kings, the auxiliaries, and the general population.

The Forms and the Good

What Is a Form?

- Introduces the concept of metaphysics: Theories about the nature of reality.

- Defines the theory of Forms. Examples: The perfect circle; the form of Bed. Asks whether there are forms for negatives.

AUTHOR'S TIP

The theory of Forms is difficult to understand for beginners in philosophy. I have had some success approaching the subject by explaining that at Plato's time the Greek intellectuals did not think in terms of *concepts* of language, as we might, but of *entities*; it is only a short distance to the mythological period where deifying concepts was customary, as in the case of the goddess Nike (Victory). Plato's form of the Good can be seen as a nontheological version of the same phenomenon.

The Form of the Good

- A hierarchy of forms is presented.

- The Theory of Forms is illustrated by Plato's Myth of the Cave.

- The Platonic legacy in Christianity.

AUTHOR'S TIP

If your students are receptive you may want to introduce them to the "third man" problem; I did not include it in the text because I found that it took the reader too far from the general topic of virtue. The "third man" criticizes Plato's Forms for ending in an infinite regress of Forms. It assumes that Plato's theory of Forms rests on the assumption that the Forms are *like* their

---

copies in the tangible world. The Form of Beauty is beautiful, the Form of a puppy looks like a generic puppy. You may try an example along these lines (the "third man" is usually only grasped easily by a few students in a lower division class): If two cats are both identified as cats, Plato would say, it is because they both participate in the Form Cat, in "catness," so to speak. So in order to compare two things (like two cats), we need a third thing (a "third man," like the Form Cat) to compare them with. But how can we tell that one cat (cat_1) and the Form Cat (Cat_2) are alike? There must be some higher Form of Cat (Cat_3) with which we compare cat_1 and Cat_2. And how do we know that Cat_3 is like cat_1 and Cat_2? There must be an even higher Form, Cat_4, that serves as a basis of comparison, and so forth. You may want to mention to your students that Aristotle considered this such a serious blow to the theory of Forms that he, himself, abandoned the Platonic idea that Forms are separate from things, and held that there are Forms, but they are embedded in the world of things, existing as the cause that make things retain their shape and identity (the formal cause). Aristotle's theory of causes will be mentioned in Chapter 9.

Primary Reading

- Plato's *Apology,* excerpts. In the first section Socrates argues against the accusation that he has corrupted the youth of Athens. In the second he defends his way of life.

Narratives

- *A Man for All Seasons,* film (1966), summary. In this true story from England of Henry VIII, Sir Thomas More refuses to support his king in the questions of the king's divorce. More acts according to his conscience, but is accused of treason, and eventually executed. The story is used to draw parallels between the trial of Socrates and that of More.

- Robert Sheckley, "The Store of the World," short story (1959), summary and excerpt. This science fiction story illustrates the question of what constitutes a good life. Mr. Wayne is given the opportunity to live an alternative version of history for a year. He chooses to live the everyday life with his family which was taken away from him by atomic war.

- Plato, "The Myth of the Cave," the *Republic,* excerpt. In this excerpt Plato tells about the cave where prisoners are kept chained so all they perceive are shadows on a wall, and speculates what might happen to a person who saw the truth and let others know. The story is used not only to illustrate Plato's theory of forms, but to draw a connection to the death of Socrates.

- *Cyrano de Bergerac,* film (1990), based on Rostand's novel, summary. This classic narrative about the unappreciated poet with the large proboscis is used to draw parallels between Plato's philosophy of the all-importance of the soul and the unimportance of physical existence.

SOME ADDITIONAL NARRATIVES ILLUSTRATING THE PLATONIC VIEW OF
APPEARANCE AND REALITY (TO FIND TRUE REALITY ONE MUST LEARN
TO LOOK BENEATH THE SURFACE)

Victor Hugo, *The Hunchback of Notre Dame*, novel (1831), film
(1939), cartoon (1996)

Beauty and the Beast, film (1946)

The Conformist, film (1970)

Being There, film (1979)

My Left Foot, film (1989)

Dogfight, film (1963)

The Man Without a Face, film (1993)

The Return of Martin Guerre, film (1983)

Boxes

8.1   *Victims of Fanaticism* The murder of Hypatia, and the burning of the library at
Alexandria.

8.2   *The Tripartite Soul: Plato and Freud* A comparison between Plato's theory of
the three parts of the soul and Sigmund Freud's theory of the Id, the Ego, and
the Superego.

8.3   *Three Theories of Metaphysics* Introduces the concepts of materialism,
idealism, and dualism.

8.4   *The Theory of Anamnesis* Presents Plato's theory of anamnesis and connects it
with the concept of reincarnation.

Chapter 9: Aristotle's Virtue Theory

- The extent of Aristotle's role in philosophy is outlined, including his
concept of teleology and causation. In particular his theory of virtue is
examined with examples. The chapter concludes with an overall discussion
of virtue theory.

Main Points

Aristotle the Scientist

Empirical Knowledge and the Realm of the Senses

- Aristotle's life and influence as a philosopher and a scientist.

Life, the Universe, and Everything

- The importance of logic and observation for Aristotle; his intellectual interests in ethics, metaphysics, politics, drama, rhetorics, etc.

Teleology: The Concept of Purpose

- Aristotle's theory that everything has a purpose.

Aristotle and the Virtues

Virtue and Excellence

- For Aristotle "virtue" means doing something with excellence.

Is There a Human Purpose?

- The telos for humans as a species, and the telos for an individual person, both are defined by that specie's or person's potential.
- The human purpose is to use one's reason well.
- Aristotle's two forms of virtue: Intellectual and moral.

The Virtues

- The Golden Mean: Not too much, and not too little.

AUTHOR'S TIP

Many students seem to think that Aristotle by his theory of the Golden Mean is praising mediocrity, or is envisioning some bland average as a moral ideal. You may want to emphasize that on the contrary Aristotle praises excellence as virtuous, and that requires the best possible effort. But the "best" effort is not the same as the "most" effort: That would be in excess. Aristotle believes it is virtuous to know when an effort is sufficient; you may want to ask your students for examples from personal experience (such as putting the right amount of effort into studying for an exam, writing a term paper, or—on a personal level—being the right kind of friend). The best possible (virtuous) result is far from being an average result; also, the question of "what is the right amount" is something most people have to face continually: How grateful should I be? How friendly? How assertive? There is no question of seeking the average, but the best, response in each situation. The question of gratitude is explored further in Chapter 12.

- Discussion of three questions about Aristotle's virtue theory: (1) If this is supposed to be a theory of character, why does Aristotle talk about conduct? (2) What does developing a good character have to do with rational thinking? (3) Are we supposed to do everything in the right amount, such as stealing and lying?

- The Golden Mean is relative to the situation.

- Discussion of examples of Aristotle's virtues: Courage, temperance, pride, being even-tempered, truthfulness, wit.

- Two dispositions of vice, with virtue in the middle: How does one find the virtue? By trial and error, and developing good habits.

Happiness

- Aristotle's idea of well-being: contemplation.

- The death of Aristotle, and the fate of his school and his ideas.

- Asking the question: Was Aristotle himself in the end courageous, i.e., virtuous?

Some Objections to Greek Virtue Theory

- The advantage of ethics of conduct over virtue ethics: Recourse to a common law.

- Virtue ethics is based in teleology, and we can't make assumptions about natural human purposes.

Primary Reading

Aristotle, *Nicomachean Ethics*, excerpt. Here Aristotle defines what he means by courage, rashness, and cowardice.

Narratives

- *Lord Jim* (film, 1965, based on Joseph Conrad's novel from 1900), summary: A young officer in the British Mercantile Marine believes himself to be destined for heroic deeds, but when the time for testing comes, he succombs to his fear of death and abandons ship during a storm, leaving the passengers to fend for themselves. For the rest of his life he engages in acts of bravery to atone for his act of cowardice.

- The Islandic epic of *Njal's Saga* (ca.1280 C.E.), excerpt. Njal and his wife Bergthora with their grandchild are held prisoners in their farmhouse by their blood-feud enemies, and Bergthora and the child choose to face death with Njal rather than to accept the enemy's offer of safety.

- "The Fall of Icarus" (ancient Greek myth), summary. The great artisan Daedalus and his son Icarus flee the island of Crete on wings fashioned by Daedalus from feathers and wax. Daedalus admonishes his son not to fly too high, or too low, but Icarus soars too close to the sun, the wax melts, and he plunges to his death. The story is used here as an illustration of the Aristotelian principle of moderation as a virtue.

> ## AUTHOR'S TIP
>
> The famous painting by Bruegel, *The Fall of Icarus*, reflects not only Greek mythology but also the Roman poet Ovid's retelling. Thus, the figures of the shepherd, the sailor, the fisherman, and the ploughman are all mentioned by Ovid. The feeling of nature's utter indifference to Icarus' plight which we find in this painting, according to art historians, mirrors Bruegel's own view of the loneliness of the life of the artist. Bruegel has included something which apparently refers to an old Flemish proverb, by adding a hint of a dead body in the bushes on the left: The proverb "The plough goes over cadavers." The partridge on the right is straight out of Ovid, however: The bird used to be Daedalus's old teacher, whom he threw off a tower, but the goddess Minerva (Athena) transformed him into a bird during his fall. The fall of Icarus is thus also the teacher's revenge.

SOME ADDITIONAL STORIES ILLUSTRATING
THE THEMES OF COURAGE AND COWARDICE

H. C. Andersen, "The Little Mermaid," fairy tale (1837)

The Lives of a Bengal Lancer, film (1935)

Ernest Hemingway, *For Whom the Bell Tolls*, novel (1940), film (1943)

This Land is Mine, film (1943)

The Red Badge of Courage, film (1951)

The Bridge on the River Kwai, film (1957)

They Came to Cordura, film (1959)

633 Squadron, film (1964)

Khartoum, film (1966)

Seven Women, film (1966)

Masada, television miniseries (1980)

A Love in Germany, film (1984)

Backdraft, film (1991)

Courage Under Fire, film (1996)

Star Trek: Deep Space Nine, "Now the Battle to the Strong," television episode (1996)

SOME ADDITIONAL NARRATIVES ILLUSTRATING ARISTOTLE'S VIRTUE
THEORY IN GENERAL (THE GOLDEN MEAN)

Jane Austen, *Sense and Sensibility*, novel (1811), film (1995)

Carlito's Way, film (1993)

Boxes

9.1 *The Four Causes* Aristotle's theory of causation: Material, efficient, formal, and final causes.

9.2 *Teleological Explanation* Discusses a teleological type of explanation vs. a causal explanation.

9.3 *Is There a Human Purpose?* Two other thinkers reflecting on the theme of human purpose: Saint Thomas Aquinas and Jean-Paul Sartre.

9.4 *The Right Decision at the Right Time* Example of Aristotle's virtue theory: three women on a bridge watching a child being swept downriver. One is cowardly, one is rash, and one is courageous.

9.5 *The Clash Between Classical and Christian Virtues* A comparison between Aristotle's list of virtues and the traditional Christian list of cardinal virtues and cardinal sins.

9.6 *Variations on Aristotle's Theme of the Golden Mean* An Aristotelian-style list of virtues and corresponding vices that aren't included on Aristotle's list.

Chapter 10: Modern Perspectives

This chapter looks at modern virtue theory, first in the new American tradition represented by the philosophers Bernard Mayo, Philippa Foot, and Christina Hoff Sommers, and secondly within the modern Continental tradition of the quest for authenticity. The philosophers represented here are Søren Kierkegaard, Martin Heidegger, Jean-Paul Sartre, and Emmanuel Levinas.

Main Points

A Revival of Virtue Theory

- Explores some strengths and weaknesses of virtue ethics, and the difference between a morality of virtue and an ethics of virtue. ("Morality" moralizes, and "ethics" questions).

AUTHOR'S TIP

You may want to show your students that the debate between virtue ethics and ethics of conduct is played out on a regular basis these years, in every recent election year. The questions of "character" versus "issues" in many

---

ways parallel the virtue vs. conduct discussion: Should we focus on a candidate's character, or should we focus on what he or she has accomplished (or says he or she will accomplish)? You may want to ask your students to find examples of this in the political debate. While the last elections of the twentieth century in this country generally had Republicans focus on character and Democrats focus on issues, it is by no means certain that the parties will align themselves similarly in the future.

Have Virtue, and Then Go Ahead

Bernard Mayo

- Mayo: If we have a set of virtues, we usually choose the right conduct; however, ethics of conduct does not guarantee that one becomes a good person, only that one does right.

- Exemplars should be emulated.

AUTHOR'S TIP

Here you may want to engage your students in a discussion of who they might nominate as role models. In such a discussion disagreements about who might qualify as a role model will probably serve well to illustrate several, perhaps all, of the following three criticisms. Of names coming up in my class discussions with regularity I can mention Jane Goodall, Bill Gates, and Hillary Rodham Clinton.

- Three criticisms of the role model idea: (1) Who decides what is a suitable role model? (2) What if one's chosen role model turns out to have serious flaws? (3) Merely imitating others is not authentic behavior.

Philippa Foot

- Foot: Virtues are not merely dispositions that we can't be held accountable for, but a matter of intention—a good will to correct a tendency to go astray.

- Are naturally virtuous people as morally praiseworthy as people who make an effort to overcome a bad inclination? Foot claims that naturally virtuous people are morally superior.

- A Kantian response to Foot's argument.

Christina Hoff Sommers

- Sommers's argument for teaching virtues in classrooms in order to avoid the spread of ethical subjectivism.

- There are moral values that can't be disputed, such as avoiding "to think only of yourself, to steal, to lie, to break promises."

- Sommers's call to a strengthening of moral values is evaluated and criticized, because an element is missing: Arguments in support of virtues based on reason.

The Quest for Authenticity

- The virtue of authenticity in the continental tradition of existentialism: Kierkegaard, Heidegger, Sartre, and Levinas.

Kierkegaard

The life and influence of Søren Kierkegaard, and his emotional ties to his father.

- Kierkegaard's quote from *Stages on Life's Way* concerning his father.

- The feeling of angst (anguish, dread) at having to make choices.

- The concept of the subjectivity of truth: Only the individual can reach what is the truth for him or her. It can't be adopted from someone else.

- The theory of the three stages in life: The aesthetic stage, the ethical stage, and the religious stage, reached by a leap of faith.

Heidegger's Intellectual Authenticity

- Martin Heidegger's theory of human existence as a fundamental interaction with the world. The term for humans: "Being-There" (*Dasein*).

- The inauthentic situations for humans happen when they let themselves believe that they are merely things affected by circumstances. Authenticity is gained when humans take responsibility, choose to think for themselves, and realize they can interact with the world and affect it.

- Heidegger's concept of anguish: The realization that all human concerns and rules are relative and that there is no absolute truth.

- Evaluation of Heidegger's concept of authenticity: Merely a call to reexamine ourselves ("getting in touch with ourselves"), or a constant state of intellectual open-mindedness?

Sartre's Ethical Authenticity

- A presentation of Jean-Paul Sartre's role in the existential movement.

- Since there are no objective values, according to existentialism, life is absurd. This means that humans can create their own values through the process of choice, and only through choosing can one attain authenticity.

- Anguish is felt at the moment of choice, and may lead to the inauthenticity of deluding oneself that one does not have to choose because one has no options. This is known as "bad faith."

- Example of bad faith: The young woman on a date who thinks she can avoid choosing whether or not she wants a physical relationship with her date.

- Humans can't avoid choosing: We are condemned to be free.

- Authenticity depends on your accomplishments, and not what you intended to do but never got done.

- Sartre and the Other: A game of dominance.

AUTHOR'S TIP

At this point you may consider discussing whether or not the continental concern for authenticity qualifies as an example of virtue ethics. An argument in favor would be that Anglo-American virtue ethics is concerned with building up a good character, and integrity and responsibility (authenticity) can also be considered important elements of a good character. An argument against accepting theories of moral authenticity as part of a general virtue theory would focus on the issue of role models. Anglo-American virtue theory approves of role models as exemplars to

---

follow, whereas the existentialist search for authenticity precludes merely following the example of other people: Emulating others could be seen as a way to avoid taking full responsibility for one's own life and situation—in other words, bad faith. It may interest your students to resume the discussion from the Bernard Mayo section and apply it to the entire discussion of authenticity: Is it possible to be authentic and have role models, too? Must authenticity imply acting without inspiration from others? Can a middle way be found?

Levinas and the Face of the Other

- Similarities and differences between Sartre and Levinas.

- Presentation of Levinas's idea of ethics as first philosophy: One's own existence is subordinate to that of the Other.

- The role of the face: The asymmetrical situation of the encounter with the Other, and one's response to the other.

- The ultimate disregard for the Other is epitomized by the Nazi Holocaust.

- Levinas's concept of autonomy finds integrity in one's relationship to another person; as such, Levinas comes closest of all modern European philosophers to an ethic of virtue.

- Levinas and feminist reactions: In his early works, Levinas identifies female nature as the Other, which has caused feminists like Simone de Beauvoir to label him as reactionary. However, new feminists read a positive meaning into his later statements.

Primary Readings

- Søren Kierkegaard, *Johannes Climacus* (1842–43, published 1913), excerpt. In this section Kierkegaard lets Johannes experience a childhood that closely resembles his own.

- Søren Kierkegaard, *Either/Or,* (1843) excerpt. Here Judge Williams admonishes his friend, a Don Juan type, about the importance of making moral choices.

- T. Wright, P. Hughes, A. Ainlix, "An Interview With Emmanuel Levinas," excerpt. This text focuses on Levinas's theory of the face. The graduate student interviewers ask questions of Levinas about whether the face can be completely defined, whether language is a necessity in order to understand another as a face, and whether animals can have faces in an ethical sense.

Narratives

Because of the many themes within this chapter, there are five Narratives to choose from:

- Woody Allen's film *Hannah and Her Sisters* (1986), summary of an episode. This section of the film illustrates the true existential angst of the hypochondriac; when the time comes that he may actually have a fatal disease, he is paralyzed with fear. The fear turns to existential angst, however, when he learns that he is not ill after all. Instead of feeling relieved, he realizes that nothing is certain, and that sooner or later he will die; now he truly faces the meaninglessness of life.

- Jean-Paul Sartre's play *No Exit* (1944), summary. This narrative deals with three characters, a man and two women, doomed to spend an eternal afterlife in each other's company, each agonizing over the things they did in life, and worse, over the things they did not do. We use it here to discuss the existential idea that your intentions only count when you have attempted to realize them.

- *A Few Good Men*, film (1992), summary. A young marine dies after being attacked by fellow marines, and two young navy lawyers investigate the matter. The question is whether the attack was a "Code Red," a disciplinary action taken to punish the marine, ordered by a superior officer. The story is used to discuss the existential claim that "I was just following orders" is always a bad excuse.

- Karen Blixen's novella *Babette's Feast* (1953), film (1988), summary. The novella tells of a Frenchwoman, a long-term refugee from the French Revolution, showing her gratitude to the two elderly sisters who took her in by spending her inheritance, treating them and their fundamentalist Christian congregation to a superb French dinner, and through this culinary masterpiece she regains her identity as a master-chef. This story is used to discuss the nature of ego-integrity.

- Iris Murdoch's novel *The Good Apprentice* (1985), summary. This narrative follows the agonies of Edward who has caused his friend's death and can find no peace with himself, even if few others blame him. Through an inner journey Edward comes to grips with himself and his guilt. The story relates to both existential authenticity and the character-development of virtue-theory.

SOME ADDITIONAL NARRATIVES ILLUSTRATING THE FEELING OF EXISTENTIAL ANGUISH AND THE ABSURDITY OF LIFE

Ernest Hemingway, *The Sun Also Rises*, novel (1926), film (1957, much better than the 1984 television version)

Franz Kafka, "The Metamorphosis," short story (1915); *The Trial*, novel (1935)

Berdil Malmberg, *Ake and His World,* "The Tail," short story (1937)

Albert Camus, *The Stranger*, novel (1942), film (1967)

Samuel Beckett, *Waiting for Godot*, play (1954)

John Irving, *The World According to Garp*, novel (1978), film (1982)

Zentropa, film (1992)

The Exterminating Angel, film (1962)

SOME ADDITIONAL NARRATIVES ILLUSTRATING
AUTHENTICITY AND EGO INTEGRITY

Leo Tolstoi, *War and Peace*, novel (1864–69), film (1956, 1968)

Romain Rolland, *Jean Christophe*, novel (1905-12)

Thomas Hardy, *Far from the Madding Crowd*, novel, film (1967)

Design for Living, film (1933)

Somerset Maugham, *The Razor's Edge*, novel (1943), film (1946). Don't bother with the 1984 version.

The Man Who Shot Liberty Valence, film (1962)

Harry and Tonto, film (1974)

Star Wars, film (1977)

Local Hero, film (1983)

Children of a Lesser God, film (1986)

John Irving, *A Prayer for Owen Meany,* novel (1989)

City Slickers, film (1991)

Leaving Normal, film (1992)

Thunderheart, film (1992)

Groundhog Day, film (1993)

Beyond Rangoon, film (1995)

Mr. Holland's Opus, film (1995)

Boxes

10.1   *Can We Change Our Spots?* Discusses whether we are responsible for our character and dispositions; virtue ethics claims we can improve on our character.

10.2   *Negative Role Models* Virtue-ethics often focuses on heroes and saints, but important moral lessons in virtue are also learned from negative role models; examples of real and fictional characters who serve as negative role models.

10.3   *Kant and Role Models* Kant rejects the idea of choosing people to emulate, for the psychological reason that humans often tend to resent those they can't measure up against. Typical situation: Parents holding one child up as a model for the other child.

AUTHOR'S TIP

The boxes on negative role models and Kant's view on role models may serve as a good topic for a class discussion. In all probability many of your students have heard siblings praised as models to emulate. Are proponents of virtue-ethics right when they claim that we can learn more easily from positive and negative role models than from rules of conduct, or is Kant right that being exposed to role models breeds resentment? You may want your students to evaluate whether they themselves generally learn most from positive role models, negative role models, or rules of conduct.

10.4 *MacIntyre and the Virtues* Alasdair MacIntyre's theory of the importance of cultural tradition in a value theory.

10.5 *A Kind of Love, and A Marriage that Wasn't: Regine Olsen.* The story of Kierkegaard's relationship with Regine Olsen, and his attempts to make her break off the engagement.

10.6 *Heidegger and the Nazi Connection* Heidegger's relationship to his teacher Edmund Husserl, and Heidegger's role during the Nazi reign in Germany.

10.7 *Nietzsche and Existentialism* A brief introduction to Friedrich Nietzsche and his influence on French existentialism; Nietzsche's statement, "God is dead," and his analysis of master- and slave moralities are introduced.

10.8 *Henri Bergson: Let Your True Self Emerge* Bergson's theory of time and free will is briefly outlined. For Bergson, the experience of our true self happens as a break-through experience when we act in a way we had not expected ourselves to act. The deeper self emerges in spite of customs and reason. Bergson's life and death are briefly described.

10.9 *The Art of Being Human* The concept of ego integrity, coined by Erik Erikson. Psychologists recognize the concept of authenticity in resolving crisis situations. Persons with ego integrity take responsibility for their actions but don't agonize over things they have no control over.

10.10 *Levinas, Kierkegaard, and Abraham* The discussion of the story of Abraham and Isaac from Chapter 2 is resumed here, with the addition of Levinas's interpretation of the story, and his criticism of Kierkegaard's version.

Chapter 11: Different Gender, Different Ethic?

This chapter raises the question of whether there are major morally relevant differences between women and men, and whether women and men approach moral problems differently. A connection between feminism and virtue-ethics is drawn, and the contemporary debates on feminism are shown to branch off in two major directions: One which views men and women as persons first and foremost (represented by Beauvoir), and one which sees men and women as fundamentally different, but equal (represented by Gilligan).

Feminism and Virtue Theory

- A definition of classical feminism as a quest for equality and non-discrimination.

- Modern virtue-ethics has become an alternative to the rules of deontology and utilitarianism and their implicit ideal of impartiality. The modern feminist virtue-ethics has become known as ethics of care, as opposed to the traditional ethics of justice.

What Is Gender Equality?

Gender and Language

- The shift from gender-specific to gender-neutral language is outlined and discussed.

AUTHOR'S TIP

As you may be aware, Dr. Virginia Warren of California State University, Long Beach has authored a guide to avoidance of gender-specific terms in the field of philosophy, published by the APA. I have used these guidelines myself as an instructional device when discussing term papers and essay tests with my students, and for many students it is an eye-opening process. The idea that language can affect one's thinking (that gender-specific terms may subconsciously affect one's outlook on gender equality) is novel to many students, and a class discussion on the subject is usually a lively experience.

Is Biology Destiny?

- Two questions are implied: (1) Is there cultural/social equality? (normative) and (2) is there biological equality? (descriptive).

- Discussing physical and intellectual biological equality through the concept of sexual dimorphism and recent brain research.

- Suggesting abandoning the idea of actual (descriptive) equality for making a policy based on normative equality: What we would like to see happen. Otherwise we may be committing the naturalistic fallacy.

Women's Historic Role in the Public Sector

- Women's traditional role in the private sphere, and lack of influence in the public sphere.

- Working-class women have usually had a closer connection to the public sphere than middle- and upper-class women, but without public recognition or equality.
- The duality of men protecting women and regarding them as property.

Early Feminism in France and England

- The French pre-revolution debate introduced by Poulain de la Barre, a student of Descartes; revolution-era support from Madame d'Epinay, but without great following: The prevailing revolutionary view sided with Rousseau, that women belonged at home.
- In eighteenth-century England Mary Wollstonecraft argued for equal rights of women, including the right to an education.
- In nineteenth-century England John Stuart Mill and Harriet Taylor argued that both men's and women's character is molded by society.

The Two Facets of Gender Equality

- A brief history of Western feminism in the twentieth century.
- A shift in feminism from a focus on access to jobs and equal pay to a focus on women's special qualities.

Men and Women Are Persons

- Classical feminism is represented by Simone de Beauvoir: Woman is seen by man, and by herself "the Other," an atypical person, and the only way women can become authentic persons is to leave their role as deviant human beings through receiving the same education and treatment as men receive. When that happens, most of the gender differences will disappear.
- The consequence: Androgynism as a political ideal. Joyce Trebilcot: Monoandrogynism (everyone in a society ought to share all the best characteristics of both genders) rejected in favor of polyandrogynism (everyone in a society is free to choose his or her gender role).
- An ultimate version of androgynism: Changing human biology through surgery.
- Research with children is inconclusive: When children are treated in a gender-neutral way, some opt for playing gender-neutral games or games typical of the opposite sex, but most seem to choose the traditional games of their own sex.

Men and Women Are Fundamentally Different

- The new feminism focuses on the fundamental differences between men and women and seeks a reevaluation in favor of women's qualities.

- Key argument: Science has treated man as the typical human being and woman as deviant or nonexistent. Both genders ought to be equally representative of the human race, including their differences.

- Carol Gilligan as representative of the new feminism: Men and women have different moral attitudes, and one is as correct as the other. Men tend toward an ethics of justice and rights, while women tend toward an ethics of caring.

- The Heinz dilemma as illustration of Gilligan's point.

- The "caring imperative": Gilligan's theory is interpreted as normative rather than descriptive.

- A critical analysis of the consequences of Gilligan's theory: It may polarize the gender issue and make it harder for women to achieve equality in the workplace, and it may result in discrimination against male qualities.

Primary Reading

- Carol Gilligan, *In A Different Voice* (1982), excerpt. In this excerpt Gilligan criticizes Erikson's theory of childhood development, and uses examples by Bettelheim of male and female psychology through two fairy tales.

Narratives

- Henrik Ibsen, *A Doll's House*, play (1879), excerpts and summary. Torvald Helmer regards his wife Nora as another child, and is oblivious to the desperate situation she has placed herself in in order to help him: She has forged a signature in order to obtain a loan, and now a disgruntled ex-employee of her husband's threatens to expose her. In the end, when Torvald knows everything and yet understands nothing of her motivations, and persists in treating her as a minor, she leaves him. The story is used to compare ethics of justice and ethics of care.

- Laura Esquivel, *Like Water for Chocolate*, novel (1989), film (1992), summary. Tita is in love with Pedro, but according to her mother Tita must, as the youngest daughter, forego all thoughts of marriage and children, because her duty is to stay and take care of her mother for as long as she lives. In order to stay close to his beloved, Pedro marries Tita's older sister. The story is used to discuss family duties and ethics of care.

- *Thelma and Louise,* film (1991), summary. This influential film tells of two women who, due to a set of unforeseen circumstances, find themselves on the road to being criminals. During their car ride from Arkansas to New Mexico they face questions of their own identity and roles as women. The story is used to discuss gender roles.

SOME ADDITIONAL NARRATIVES ILLLUSTRATING THE QUESTION OF GENDER ROLES

August Strindberg, *Getting Married,* play (1884)

Adam's Rib, film (1949)

Seven Women, film (1966)

Masculine Feminine, film (1966)

Alice Walker, *The Color Purple*, novel (1982) and film (1985)

Swing Shift, film (1984)

Pamels Sargent, *The Shore of Women,* novel (1986)

Margaret Atwood, *A Handmaid's Tale*, novel (1985). Better than the film.

Sheri S. Tepper, *The Gate to Women's Country,* novel (1988)

Sheri S. Tepper, *Raising the Stones*, novel (1990)

He Said, She Said, film (1991)

Mi Vida Loca, My Crazy Life, film (1994)

Oleanna, play and film, 1994. Some critics point out that the play is superior to the film.

Boys on the Side, film (1995)

Terry McMillan, *Waiting to Exhale*, novel (1993), film (1995)

Antonia's Line, film (1996)

SOME STORIES WITH A TWIST TO THE GENDER SUBJECT

Some Like It Hot, film (1939)

La Cage Aux Folles, film (1978)

Yentl, film (1983)

The Crying Game, film (1992)

Star Trek: The Next Generation: "The Outcast," television episode (1992). An androgynous society discriminating against heterosexual behavior.

The Bird Cage, film (1996)

To Wong Foo, Thanks for Everything, Julie Newmar, film (1995)

Boxes

11.1   *Sex or Gender?* An explanation of the shift in terminology from "sex" to "gender."

11.2   *The Issue Is Manhole Covers* Examples of gender-specific and gender-neutral terms are used in a discussion of how much we should change our terminology.

11.3   *Women Moral Philosophers* A short list of women thinkers from antiquity to the early twentieth century who have made their mark on moral philosophy.

11.4   *What Is Sexual Harassment?* A list provided by the Fair Employment and Housing Act defining situations of sexual harassment. A subsequent discussion of possible interpretations of the list.

11.5   *The Other: Simone de Beauvoir* A biography of Beauvoir, an evaluation of her philosophical connection with Sartre, and an evaluation of her role in the recent feminist debate.

11.6   *Can Gays Choose Not to Be Gay?* A discussion of whether homosexuality is a matter of biology or a choice of lifestyle. Tentative scientific results point toward it being a biological phenomenon. Consequences for the debate are outlined.

11.7   *Rifts in Today's Feminism* A discussion of Christina Hoff Sommers's claim in *Who Stole Feminism* that feminism has been split into two movements: The "equity feminists" and the "gender feminists."

Chapter 12: Virtues, Values, and Religion

This chapter provides an introduction to a selection of moral viewpoints of virtue and conduct related to religious traditions past and present. The viewpoints selected fall into three groups: Asian traditions, including the ethics of Confucius and Mencius, and Buddhism; the three monotheistic religions of Islam, Judaism, and Christianity; and Tribal Virtues and Values, including the moral views of the Vikings, African virtue theory, and Native American values.

Main Points

Two Asian Traditions

- Some of the great religious and ethical systems of the world were developed over a period of six hundred years.

Confucius and Mencius

- Confucius's theory of a man of virtue: Someone who is wise, courageous, and humane, and who strives to develop good habits and continual good thinking.

- Confucian virtue theory of *te, jen, li,* and *yi.*

- Mencius's theory that humans are born morally good, and lose their goodness through bad influence. Development of one's character and recapturing one's lost goodness is virtuous.

- Mencius citation: Care of parents and developing of character as moral duties.

Buddhism

- The life of Siddhartha Gautama

- The concept of enlightenment, and the Four Noble Truths: (1) Life is suffering, (2) suffering is caused by craving for life, (3) if craving ceases, suffering will cease, and (4) the way to stop craving is to follow the Noble Eightfold Path.

- An analysis of the Buddhist concept of suffering (*dukkha*).

- Buddhism is an example of Asian ethics of conduct, while Confucianism is an example of Asian virtue-ethics.

Virtues, Values, and Conduct in Three Monotheistic Religions

Islam

- A brief history of Islam.

- A description of some of the most important doctrines of Islam: The view of reality, free will, and the sin of disobedience.

- Two Islamic interpretations of fate.

- Islamic virtue-theory and its relation to Aristotle. The true problem is seen by Islam as the weakness of a person's character.

Judaism

- A brief history of Judaism; three areas of interest in ethics: Ethics of conduct, metaethcics, and virtue-ethics.

- Four components of ethical monotheism: (1) God's laws are binding on everyone; (2) God's laws protect everyone; (3) the moral standards apply to everyone, including God; and (4) human freedom and dignity are very important.

- The philosophy of Moses Maimonides: The importance of wisdom, and the doctrine of the four levels of perfection. Similarities and differences between Maimonides and Aristotle.

- The tradition of charity and compassion.

- Modern Judaism: Buber and Levinas.

Christianity

- The influences on the historical development of Christianity.

- Recap of Chapter 8: The claim that Christianity brought a halt to ancient virtue-ethics is put into a new context of the Christian tradition. Christian virtue-ethics is subordinate to ethics of conduct.

- Two major sources of Catholic theology: St. Augustine and St. Thomas Aquinas.

- Augustine's interpretation of the original sin.

- Aquinas's interpretation of the intellect as a God-given tool.

- Natural law theory as a Thomistic legacy. Thomistic ethics is teleological.

- The various moral focal points of Protestant ethics.

Tribal Virtues and Values

The Virtues of the Vikings

- The historical background for the Viking tradition and its persistence well into Christian times.

- The tradition of justice among equals, loyalty to family and friends, honor in battle, and trusting in one's good luck.

- The current popularity of Viking folklore.

- The status of women and slaves in Viking society.

African Virtue-Theory

- The virtue ethics of the Akan people in West Africa: A communitarian ethic seen by the Akan people as having a humanistic origin, with a natural law approach.

- Belief: A good character is acquired through good habits.

- Virtues are taught through storytelling, habituating the children to moral virtues.

- The most important ideal of Akan ethics is the well-being of the community.

Native American Values

AUTHOR'S TIP

Referring to the original inhabitants of the North American continent is becoming increasingly controversial; the term *Indian* is unacceptable to many, since it is indeed a misnomer; however, many Native Americans prefer to refer to themselves as Indians, adding their tribal affiliation (such as Lakota Indian). Scholars have for years used the term *American Indian*, but it is still tainted by the misconceptions of the era of Columbus. *Native*

American has become an established term in the non-Indian communities as a recognition of the people of the tribes as the original inhabitants, but many (with or without Indian tribal affiliations) don't approve of the term because it implies that non-Indian Americans are not native to their own country. Alternative terminologies are: original Americans, indigenous Americans, First Americans, and the Canadian term First Nations. After recently hearing arguments from leaders of American Indian tribes advocating the term *American Indian* I now lean toward using that term myself.

- Traditional Native American ethics involve humans, animals, and nature as a moral community. Good social relations must be maintained with all elements, according to J. Baird Callicott.

- According to Callicott the Native American tradition was not conservationist in a scientific sense, but in a moral sense: A sense of social order.

- The association of Native American values and ecological virtue is evaluated in terms of the past and the present.

Primary Readings

This section contains eight short readings from the traditions explored in this chapter:

- *Confucius Teaches the Golden Rule and the Golden Mean.* Excerpt.

- *The Buddha Speaks to His Disciples.* Excerpt.

- *Sura XLIX, The Apartments, the Qur'an.* Excerpt.

- *Isaiah 1:11–17.* Excerpt.

- *St. Luke 6:27–38.* Excerpt.

- *The Words of the High One (Havamal).* Excerpt.

- *Akan Proverbs.* Excerpt.

- *Diné (Navajo) Dawn Chant.*

Narratives

- *The Arab Tradition:* "Test of Friendship," a Syrian folktale, summary. A wealthy father teaches his son how to tell a true friend from a false one by setting himself up on a false murder charge, observing the reaction of his own friends. The story is used to discuss the issue of character.

- *The Judaic Tradition:* Isaac Bashevis Singer, "A Piece of Advice," short story (1958). Summary and excerpt. Baruch's wealthy father-in-law learns to control his temper after meeting a wise Rabbi. The story is used to discuss conduct and character.

- *The African Tradition:* "The Quality of Friendship," an African folktale from the Vai tribe, summary. A young man who is visited by a friend is swallowed by a snake. The friend rescues him, but loses his sight in the process. In order to restore his friend's sight, the young man must kill his son and smear his blood on the blinded man's face. The story is used to discuss the nature of friendship.

- *The Native American Tradition:* "White Buffalo Woman," a Lakota Sioux myth, summary and excerpt. A young woman comes from her own people, the buffalo, to the starving Lakota tribe and teaches them to hunt buffalo and smoke the sacred pipe, making all living creatures and nature one. The story is used to discuss the idea of ecological harmony.

AUTHOR'S TIP

Because of space restrictions it was not possible to include narratives from all eight traditions mentioned in this chapter, but in the text, Chapter 12, p. 430 you will find references to Narratives in other chapters that can be used to illustrate the traditions which are not represented by narratives here.

Boxes

12.1 *Confucius and Aristotle* Discusses the similarities and differences between Confucius and Aristotle.

12.2 *Taoism* A short introduction to the philosophy of Lao-Tzu, the concept of The Way, and the opposing forces of Yin and Yang.

12.3 *Karma* The Hindu doctrine of Karma and reincarnation is explored and compared with its Buddhist development.

12.4 *Fatalism* A definition of the terms fatalism, determinism, and predestination.

12.5 *Islam and the Protection of Women* An evaluation of the traditional Islamic rules restricting women's rights.

12.6 *Divine Command Theory and Natural Law* A discussion of divine command theory (something is right because God commands it) versus natural law theory (God commands it because it is right).

Chapter 13: Case Studies in Virtue

Here two virtues are selected to be examined in detail: Compassion and gratitude. Philip Hallie's account of compassion shown by a French village during World War II is presented, and Richard Taylor's view that compassion is the only virtue needed is critically examined. Next, Lin Yutang's viewpoint grounded in the Chinese tradition of gratitude toward one's parents is contrasted with Jane English's criticism of the debt-metaphor ("we owe our parents nothing"), and the concept of friendship duties is examined.

Main Points

Compassion

- In contrast to Thomas Hobbes, David Hume, Jean-Jacques Rousseau, and Mencius all agree that humans are born with compassion toward others. For Rousseau as well as for Mencius it is civilization that corrupts the original fellow-feeling.

Philip Hallie: The Case of Le Chambon

- Hallie's account of the compassion shown by a French village toward Jewish refugees during World War II.

- The concept of institutionalized cruelty, an analysis of why it happens, and how it can be helped.

Richard Taylor: Compassion Is All You Need

- Taylor's three examples of atrocities: In common for all three are malice and lack of compassion. There is no need for reason in choosing compassion.

- Taylor's three compassionate examples. Same conclusion: We don't need reason in order to be compassionate.

- Criticism of Taylor: If some humans have no compassion, reason must be used to persuade them.

- The story of *Huckleberry Finn* is used as an example of how compassion may be sufficient sometimes, but not at other times when rational judgment is needed.

AUTHOR'S TIP

It is likely that some of your students don't know the story of Huck Finn, especially if you have many exchange students or immigrant students in your class. Since it is a controversial story to some because of its use of typical nineteenth-century language, which today is identified as racist, you may want to summarize the story and spend a few minutes discussing if it is fair to criticize *Huckleberry Finn* for being a racist piece of literature. You may want to point your students' attention to the caption of the drawing of Huck and Jim: The character of Huck may have been based on an African American boy.

Gratitude—How Much, and When?

- There is a difference between feeling gratitude and showing gratitude. We can't be forced to feel something we don't feel, but we can make a show of gratitude when it is appropriate.

We Owe Our Parents Everything

- The Chinese philosopher Lin Yutang expresses the Chinese traditional belief that age deserves respect.

- According to Lin Yutang, we owe a debt of gratitude to our parents for having raised us.

- Conditions in modern China with its restrictions on childbirth, and socialized care of the elderly.

AUTHOR'S TIP

Here you may want to discuss with your students the traditions of the East and the West in terms of attitude towards the elderly. Some of your students may be of Latino or of some other ethnic, Western background that still values the elderly of a community, and it is likely that they may want to point out that a caring traditional attitude toward the elderly is not an exclusively Eastern way.

We Owe Our Parents Nothing

- Jane English claims that filial love is undermined if parents insist that their grown children are indebted to them.

- Appropriate and inappropriate ways of using the "debt-metaphor." Debts require reciprocation, while friendship duties are mutual and are not defined by past favors.

- Obligations based on love and friendship depend on (1) the need of the parents, and (2) the ability and resources of the grown child.

Friendship Duties and Gratitude

- Fred Berger's answer to questions of the extent of gratitude one ought to show: Unsolicited favors need not be reciprocated; however, if they are done for the recipient's own sake, the recipient is treated as an end in himself or herself in the Kantian sense, and gratitude is owed. If favors are done for the sake of the giver (treating the recipient as a means to an end), no gratitude is owed.

- How much gratitude should we show? The Aristotelian "right amount," varying from case to case.

How to Receive Gratitude?

- How to be a good receiver is almost as important as how to be a good giver. An Aristotelian guideline: Be willing to accept the same extent of gratitude as the extent of the favor rendered.

Virtue and Conduct: Ethical Pluralism?

- An evaluation of ethical pluralism as an example of soft universalism in practice: Allowing for a multitude of moral approaches, while seeking common agreement on some basic underlying values.

Primary Reading

- Lin Yutang, "On Growing Old Gracefully," (1937), excerpt. Lin Yutang here summarizes the Asian respect for the elderly, and the wish to serve one's parents in their old age. For the Chinese, the signs of age are positive signs. Lin Yutang criticizes the West for having abandoned the idea of mutual dependency in the home.

Narratives

- This narrative section is rather large, in order to accommodate the many themes of this chapter. It contains stories of compassion, gratitude, and a selection of stories about the two vices of jealousy and thirst for revenge. My suggestion is that you choose one story from each category to discuss with your students.

Compassion

- "The Parable of the Good Samaritan," Luke 10:30–37, summary and excerpt. A man from Samaria helps a wounded man by the wayside, while a priest and a Levite walk right by. The impact of the story depends on the reader being aware that people from Samaria were thought of as social outcasts by the Jewish community at the time. The story is used to focus on compassion.

- "King Yudisthira and the Dog," *Mahabharata*, summary. The old king walks all the way to Heaven. His companions die, and in the end only an old dog is following him. He refuses to enter Heaven without the dog. The story is used to discuss compassion toward animals as well as humans.

AUTHOR'S TIP

Study questions #2 and #4 about our emotional relationship with pets may provide a particularly engaging class discussion for your students. Since this text has focused on animal issues on several occasions, this may be a good opportunity to come full circle and talk about the issue of not only abstract rights for animals we don't know, but the extent of the "moral community" and social order that pet-owners may experience, living in a "multi-species family" with special duties and responsibilities.

- *Schindler's List*, film (1993), summary. A Polish businessman becomes engaged in saving as many Jews as possible during World War II, by hiring them as workers in his factory and, with the help of his Jewish manager, battling, bribing, and outwitting Nazi officials who are determined to send them to the death camps. In the end Schindler saved 1100 men, women, and children. The story is used to explore the issue of compassion.

SOME ADDITIONAL STORIES ILLUSTRATING THE THEME OF COMPASSION

"The Hut in the Forest," *Grimm's Fairy Tales*, short story (1812–15)

Hans Christian Andersen, *The Snow Queen,* short story (1844). The story also illustrates the issue of reason versus emotion.

Hell in the Pacific, film (1968)

Barry B. Longyear, *Enemy Mine,* short story (1979), film (1985)

Awakenings, film (1990)

Sir Walter Scott, *Ivanhoe,* novel (1820), film (1952), television version (1982)

The Fisher King, film (1991)

City of Joy, film (1992)

Forrest Gump, film (1994*)*

Red, film (1994)

ER, television series; numerous episodes

Chicago Hope, television series; numerous episodes

Gratitude

- *Eat Drink Man Woman*, film (1995), summary. This story depicts traditional Confucian values in a modern Taiwanese family: A father and three grown daughters come to terms with changes, and face their sense of obligation. The story is used to discuss Asian sense of duty toward aging parents.

- *Grand Canyon*, film (1991), summary. In this narrative Mack, a white man, is rescued from a streetgang by Simon, a black man. Afterwards, Mack wants to show his gratitude, but Simon doesn't want to receive it, because he doesn't think of his act as anything special. The story is used to discuss the art of knowing how much gratitude to show, and how to receive it.

SOME ADDITIONAL STORIES ILLUSTRATING THE THEME OF GRATITUDE

Aesop's Fables, "The Mouse and the Lion"

Charles Dickens, *Great Expectations,* novel (1860–61), film (1946)

Harold Kidde, *The Hero,* novel (1912)

It Could Happen to You, film (1994)

Jealousy

- William Shakespeare's *Othello*, play (1603–04), summary. This narrative shows the agony of the jealousy that has been planted in Othello's heart after it is maliciously and falsely suggested to him by Iago (himself jealous of Othello's success) that his wife Desdemona is having an affair with his friend Cassio. This accusation spells doom for everyone involved in the drama.

- The Pueblo Indian story of "The Warrior Maiden," summary. Red Hawk tries to break up Blue Hawk's perfect marriage by suggesting that Red Hawk's wife is unfaithful to him, and he sets out to prove it to Blue Hawk. By way of subterfuge he makes Blue Hawk believe him, and Blue Hawk puts his wife in a trunk, which he then throws in the river. She does not drown, however, but returns as a great warrior and exacts revenge on Red Hawk and forgives her husband.

Thirst for Revenge

- Alexandre Dumas's *The Count of Monte Cristo*, novel (1844). This story may be the ultimate vengeance narrative. Edmond Dantès, a young sailor about to marry the girl he loves and become captain of a ship, finds himself thrown in a dungeon with no trial on the day of his wedding, a victim of the jealousy and egoism of people he thought were his friends. Fourteen years later he escapes and seeks to destroy his victimizers through careful planning that, in the end, backfires.

- *The Searchers*, film (1956), summary. A civil war veteran, Ethan Edwards, searches for his only living relative, his niece, Debbie, who has been kidnapped by Comanche Indians after a raid that killed her family. After eight years Ethan finds his niece, but now he seeks to kill her since he considers her contaminated from living with the Indians.

AUTHOR'S TIP

Your students may enjoy a further exploration of vices such as greed, vanity, obsession, malice, overindulgence, etc., so below you will find a listing of stories that explore not only jealousy and thirst for revenge, but also a short collection of other vices. As is the case with the other collections of stories, I welcome additional suggestions of titles from readers.

SOME ADDITIONAL NARRATIVES ILLUSTRATING JEALOUSY, THIRST FOR REVENGE, AND OTHER VICES

Jealousy

Leave Her to Heaven, film (1945)

Fay Weldon, *The Life and Loves of a She-Devil,* novel (1983). Never mind the 1989 film, but the British television series was interesting.

Fatal Attraction, film (1987)

Revenge

William Shakespeare, *Hamlet,* play (ca.1600).

Fury, film (1936)

Son of Fury (1942). No relation to *Fury*!

Shadows of Forgotten Ancestors, film (1964)

High Plains Drifter, film (1973)

Death Wish, film (1974)

Star Trek II, The Wrath of Khan, film (1982)

Fay Weldon, *The Life and Loves of a She-Devil,* novel (1983)

Jean de Florette (part 1) and *Manon of the Spring* (part 2), films (1986)

Unforgiven, film (1992)

Death and the Maiden, film (1994)

Sleepers, film (1996)

An Eye for an Eye, film (1996)

First Wives' Club, film (1996)

Obsession

Thomas Mann, "Death in Venice," short story (1911), film (1971)

The Offense, film (1973)

Tightrope, film (1984)

In the Line of Fire, film (1993)

The Presence of Evil

Henry James, *The Turn of the Screw,* short story (1898)

Strangers on a Train, film (1951)

The Bad Seed, film (1956)

In Cold Blood, film (1967)

The Shining, film (1980)

Breaking the Rules

The Adventures of Don Juan, film (1948)

Tom Jones, film (1963)

Les Liaisons Dangereuses, play (1985) from story by Choderlos de *Laclos; Dangerous Liaisons,* film (1989)

Crimes and Misdemeanors, film (1989)

The Player, film (1992)

Get Shorty, film (1995)

Boxes

13.1   *Is It Better to Cry Over Your Victim Than Not to Feel Sorry?* Jonathan Bennett's claim that it is better to have compassion even if you cause death and destruction, than not to have compassion at all, is contrasted to Hallie's criticism, using an example from *Alice in Wonderland*: The Walrus and the Carpenter eating oysters.

13.2   *Compassion and Anti-Intellectualism:* Forrest Gump. The film is used here as an illustration of Taylor's claim that compassion has nothing to do with reason. The implied anti-intellectualism is discussed.

13.3   *Reason and Feeling* A variety of views on whether morality and feelings are related. An example of a fictional group of people who are unemotional but who have a strong sense of ethics.

13.4   *Love as a Virtue* Discusses whether people can actually keep promises to love one another. Suggests that we don't promise to feel passion, but to show loyalty and caring.

13.5   *Self-worth and Retirement* The Western attitude of self-worth being connected with one's usefulness and productivity is discussed.

13.6   *The Duty to Take Care of One's Parents* Filial duties in traditional societies. Reference to *Like Water for Chocolate.*

13.7   *Dating, Debt, and Friendship* English analyzes the dating situation and finds that a woman does not owe a man any favors if he takes her out as a gesture of friendship. This situation is further discussed.

13.8   *What About Relatives?* English's theory of friendship duties does not cover the situation of distant relatives in need of help.

AUTHOR'S TIP:

Since dating probably is a relevant topic for most of your students, a discussion of dating practices and sexual morality may be appropriate here, based on the box "Dating, Debt, and Friendship."

13.9   *Does the Golden Rule Always Work?* A discussion of well-meaning attempts to do unto others, when others don't want it done unto them, based on Deborah Tannen's theory on styles.

13.10   *A Short View of Vices* Aristotelian virtue theory applied to compassion and gratitude: The corresponding vices. The vices of jealousy and thirst for revenge.

Chapter 14: Conclusion: The Moral Importance of Stories

This final chapter adds a few perspectives to the role of storytelling in ethics, and concludes with two narratives about the moral and social importance of story-telling.

Stories as Survival Mechanisms

- A citation from Ilya Ehrenburg about the survival value of remembering good stories. Even within film and literature the importance of storytelling is sometimes made explicit, such as in *Fahrenheit 451*.

Martha Nussbaum: Living Other Lives

- Nussbaum is interested in the emotional value of narratives.

- Emotions have cognitive value and are, as a rule, not irrational, nor do they happen at random.

- Why have philosophers refused to deal seriously with emotions? Because when humans experience emotions they are immersed in life that affects them and can't be considered rationally autonomous.

- Emotions are our best access to values, and their clearest manifestation is in narratives.

- There are different narratives in different cultures, but this need not lead to cultural relativism.

- Why stories, and not designed philosophical examples instead? Because the rich texture of the story is what we relate to, and narratives are more open-ended than philosophical examples.

- Quote: We need stories in order to live other lives vicariously, because we have never lived enough to understand life and each other.

- Also, it is sometimes easier to discuss stories with others than talk about private moments in our own lives.

Our Stories, Our Culture

- The current revival of storytelling carries a note of urgency: Because of growing cultural diversity we need to learn about each other and each other's values through stories.

- What if the values are in conflict? Do we choose the path of ethical relativism, hard universalism, or soft universalism?

- Argument in favor of soft universalism: One should seek values to agree about, but one need not agree with all values from other cultures.

Living in the Narrative Zone

- Humans are temporal beings, living their own story between beginning and end, as well as living the stories of their culture.

- The concept of narrative time, illustrated by the story by Richard Matheson: An experience of telescoped time.

- The life-expanding experience of narrative time: We can retain our own life while sharing in the accelerated time of books and films.

- Ursula LeGuin and the metaphor of the hoop snake that bites its own tail: Storytelling is important, if it is combined with action and taking a chance, even if you may get hurt in the process.

An Afterword, and Two Final Narratives.

- Reference to the narrative summaries and excerpts in *The Moral of The Story* as illustrations of the importance of stories. Stories, experienced in the right amount, can help us make decisions and avoid mistakes.

- A suggestion to go beyond the summaries and excerpts to experience the real "narrative zone."

Narratives

- *Star Trek: Voyager*, "Prime Factor," television series episode (1995), summary. A narrative parallel to the episode "Justice" in Chapter 6, "Prime Factor" tells of the starship *Voyager,* lost in a distant part of the galaxy, attempting to purchase the technology to get home by selling copies of the starship's library of stories from all the cultures of the Federation. The episode illustrates the cultural importance of stories.

- Salman Rushdie, *Haroun and the Sea of Stories*, novel (1990), summary. In this children's story that probably can be appreciated best by adults with some political awareness, Rushdie follows in the tradition of Jonathan Swift and narrates a fable about an evil power attempting to dry out the source of storytelling. Why? Because storytelling has an uncontrollable element that the evil power can't rule over. The story illustrates the liberating element in storytelling, as a way of saving one's culture as well as oneself.

SOME ADDITIONAL NARRATIVES ILLUSTRATING
THE IMPORTANCE OF STORYTELLING

Hans Christian Andersen, "The Elfin Mound," short story, (1845)

Karen Blixen (Isak Dinesen), "The Blank Page," short story (1957)

Karen Blixen (Isak Dinesen), "The Cardinal's First Tale," short story (1957)

Ayn Rand, "The Simplest Thing in the World," short story (1967)

The French Lieutenant's Woman, film (1981)

Kim Stanley Robinson, *The Wild Shore,* novel (1984)

David Brin, *The Postman,* novel (1985)

Isabelle Allende, *Eva Luna,* novel (1987)

Jostein Gaander, *Sophia's World,* novel (1994). This book is about the history of philosophy, told within a narrative.

SUGGESTED EXAMINATION FORMATS AND TEST QUESTIONS

This section provides you with some suggestions for the format and material for objective and subjective tests.

I often hand out a sheet of information prior to a test so that the students can familiarize themselves with not only the material but also the format of the test. Such a sheet of information may look like this (reflecting my own preference for test formats):

Format for Multiple-Choice and True/False Tests (objective tests)

Examination Format

Make sure your scantron answers are clear and unambiguous; otherwise, the scantron machine cannot read them. Read the questions carefully. Total possible points: 100. **No books, no notes.**

True/False Questions: (A) = True, (B) = False. 2 points for each correct answer.

Multiple-Choice Questions: 2 points for each correct answer.

Short Essays: Answer two out of three questions. Write your answers in the Blue Book, **with a pen.** An excellent answer is worth 5 points, a very good answer gets 4 points; a not-quite-sufficient or too-short answer is worth 3 points, and a poor answer (hardly anything correct) is worth 1 point. A wrong or a blank answer gets 0. Make sure you write the numbers of each question next to your answer. Be as clear, brief, and specific as you can, and please write legibly!

Plagiarism Policy: Using open books or notes during the test, or consulting with other students, will result in an F if discovered.

Format for Essay Tests (subjective tests)

Examination Format

This will be an essay test, and you will need a Blue Book.

The following information will be on the test: Answer one [or more] of the following questions. Please write the number of the question[s] you've chosen on the **front** of your Blue Book. **No notes, no books, no pencils.**

Suggested Approach: (1) Read the questions *carefully* and choose one, (2) "brainstorm," (3) write outline, (4) write essay.

Plagiarism Policy: Using open books or notes during the test or consulting with other students will result in an F if discovered.

I tend to give essay questions with a basic structure similar to this (but more detailed):

Answer all parts of this question in the following order:

1. Describe the theory of _____ and illustrate it with examples.

2. Give an account of the criticism of this theory, using arguments from the textbook.

3. Do you agree with the theory? Explain why or why not. You may use arguments of your own.

Format of Term Papers

Format of Term Paper

[Your preferred number of pages, such as 5–8] typed, double-spaced pages. For each quote or reference you must have a footnote or endnote stating author, year, and publisher, even if you are only referring to the textbooks. Any standard reference method will be accepted. The footnotes/endnotes are *in addition to* the required pages (a page of endnotes doesn't qualify as one of the term paper pages).

HOW-TO? A good policy: Express yourself in your own words whenever possible (imagine you are explaining it to a bright friend who has never heard of it before), and save the quotes for very important phrases that you would like to leave the way the author expressed them. Don't "pad" your paper with quotes, and never put a quote in a paper without any explanation. You must follow up and explain why you think the quote is important.

A Word of Caution: Plagiarism will result in a substantial penalty, depending on the severity of the plagiarism. **What is plagiarism in a term paper?** Having someone else write the paper for you. Or copying from someone else's paper. Or copying/quoting from a book or an article without stating your source (without "reference") so that the reader thinks it is your own idea, even if you didn't intend to pass it off as your own. Even if you change a few words here and there it is still considered plagiarism!

In all such handouts before a test or a term paper, I have made it a habit to outline the criterion for plagiarism; in my experience it doesn't happen often that students plagiarize, but you may find it happening under certain circumstances: (1) The student is desperate to get a good grade and is fully aware of transgressing, (2a) the student is genuinely unaware of what constitutes plagiarism, and (2b) the student is from another country and is either used to other rules or has not understood the general rules of American schools. It is not impossible that you may encounter students from cultures that view plagiarism in a different light; in Western history, plagiarism was not considered an unscientific or unacceptable approach until well into the nineteenth century, and it is conceivable that some foreign students have grown up with a different set of values and are not aware of the severity with which we regard plagiarism today. Giving students the benefit of the doubt, you can avoid misunderstandings such as circumstances 2a and 2b by including a note about plagiarism. There is not much to be done about circumstance number 1 except make the student aware that you will give him or her a failing grade if he or she cheats.

Test Questions

The test questions follow the order of the topics in *The Moral of the Story;* however, for the most effective testing you may want to change the order and test the students on several chapters at a time, mixing up the questions.

On a few occasions I have chosen to insert a bit of humor in the objective test questions; it works well as a diffuser of tension during the test, and I doubt that it misleads the student any more than the other false options do. However, if that doesn't fit your teaching style, you are of course free to skip the "funny" options.

Having received my education within an intellectual tradition where objective tests in the humanities are nonexistent, I have certain reservations about using such tests, and I certainly want to advise against using objective tests *exclusively,* which is why I have included essay questions in each section. These essay questions can also be used as term paper questions as well as study question in a classroom context.

Grading has been made so much easier by using scantrons, but I suggest always going over the correct answers with the students and not just hand over their test results so that the false options don't get a chance to lodge in their minds forever. For the same reason I find that it is not a good idea to use too many objective questions for a final exam if there is no wrap-up meeting after the final, no matter how convenient such an arrangement may be (because objective questions are easier to grade than essay questions, and we are all pressed for time during finals week).

All primary readings and narratives are followed by study questions. These questions are also designed for use as essay questions or topics for term paper questions; some of them appear as essay questions in this section.

PART II
TEST BANK:
Objective and Essay Questions

PART II
TEST BANK
Open-ended Essay Questions

CHAPTER 1
Who Cares about Ethics?

True/False Questions

1. A misanthropic view of morals is a view that mistrusts the moral capabilities of humans. (T)

2. "Morality" usually refers to theories about the moral rules we follow. (F)

3. The Golden Rule: Do unto others before they do it to you. (F)

4. The Golden Rule: Do unto others as you would have them do unto you. (T)

5. There is common agreement among ethicists that it is not possible for an atheist to have morals. (F)

6. A nonmoral value never refers to something as being good or bad, or right or wrong. (F)

7. Legal positivism claims that the law is based on consensus, not on universal moral standards. (T)

8. Jürgen Habermas claims that scientific research is not value-free. (T)

9. Not all moral issues are relevant for lawgivers. (T)

10. Frankenstein's monster is an example of a story exploring the problem of research without a conscience. (T)

11. *Jurassic Park* illustrates the problem of scientific research without moral responsibility. (T)

12. In *Working Girl,* Tess steals her boss's idea and passes it off as her own. (F)

Multiple-Choice Questions
(Correct answers are marked with an asterisk.)

13. Which one of these answers to the question "Why are there moral rules?" is NOT in Chapter 1?
    a. Moral rules come from God/the gods.
    b. Moral rules originate in human reason.
    *c. Moral rules are dictated by the economy.
    d. Moral rules derive from the fear of being caught.

14. Which one of these descriptions comes closest to a definition of the theory of naturalism in philosophy of law?
    a. It explores the legal ramifications of nudity on beaches.
    b. It claims that any behavior that derives from human nature should be legal.
    c. It explores the natural laws of science.
    *d. It claims that the law is based on universal moral standards.

15. There are four common viewpoints to the issue of Hollywood and violent films mentioned in the text. Find the one that shouldn't be on the list.
    a. Hollywood should impose strict family values on its productions.
    *b. Hollywood is supplying a valuable social service, because we all need to watch violent films now and again.
    c. Hollywood should create more films in nonviolent categories, such as family movies.
    d. Hollywood is just responding to viewer demands.

16. There are many ways of using narratives to explore ethics. Chapter 1 mentions four ways. Which one shouldn't be on the list?
    a. Many psychologists are using bibliotherapy to make children comfortable with difficult experiences.
    b. Many medical students are exposed to literature and films about persons with illnesses in order to have a better understanding of their patients.
    *c. Many philosophy students are now reading stories about persons seeking the meaning of life in order to facilitate their own search for meaning.
    d. Stories have great potential for cross-cultural understanding.

17. In *Jurassic Park* an important question is asked: "Just because it is possible for science to do something, does that mean we ought to do it?" Who asks the question?
    *a. Malcolm, the mathematician.
    b. Gennaro, the financial adviser.
    c. Grant, the paleontologist.
    d. Sattler, the paleobotanist.

18. What is Katharine's decisive action in *Working Girl*?
    *a. She steals her assistant's idea and passes it off as her own.
    b. She promotes her assistant.
    c. She steals her assistant's boyfriend but refuses to marry him.
    d. She is Tess's assistant and steals her boss's idea.

Essay/Study Questions

19. Explain the difference between morals and ethics.

20. Give a critical evaluation of the concept "family values," with examples.

21. Why is it insufficient, according to most theories of ethics, to answer the question of what is morally right or wrong by referring to God's commands?

22. Why does Rosenstand say that the moral implications of human cloning are staggering? Can you think of some moral problems arising with the availability of such a technology?

23. Can science work in a value-free environment, or does science have a duty to work within a system of moral values?

24. Would you approve of media censorship under certain circumstances? Explain.

25. Imagine being one of the people of the future involved with DNA research; imagine it being possible, at that point in time, to actually clone creatures of the past such as dinosaurs. Would you argue in favor of this process, would you argue against it, or would you argue in favor of some other alternative? Explain.

26. Who is the worst moral transgressor in *Working Girl:* Katharine, who steals Tess's idea, or Tess, who lies to make a deal?

CHAPTER 2
Stories with Morals

True/False Questions

1. The moral of "The Boy Who Cried Wolf" is that you should never lie, because sooner or later people aren't going to believe you anymore, even when you tell the truth. (T)

2. The lesson of the story of the Little Fir Tree is that one should always save for a rainy day. (F)

3. There is a difference between stories that moralize and stories that discuss moral problems. (T)

4. A didactic story is a story that teaches a lesson. (T)

5. There is a sharp distinction between factual and fictional stories. (F)

6. Even stories that are believed to be factual have an element of poetic creativity. (T)

7. Traditional myths have two purposes: To strengthen social bonding and to serve as wish fulfillment. (F)

8. Fairy tales are, to some psychoanalysts, pure wish fulfillment. (T)

9. In "The Juniper Tree" the girl, Marjory, eats her stepmother and buries her bones under a big tree. (F)

10. The story of the prodigal son belongs to the category of parables. (T)

11. Kierkegaard believes that Abraham's obedience to God was not an example of ordinary morality, but required a leap of faith. (T)

12. We can learn moral lessons from morally good people, but not from morally flawed people. (F)

13. If one is opposed to war, one can find no moral lessons in war stories. (F)

14. The Western *Unforgiven* with Clint Eastwood provides a strong pro-violence statement. (F)

15. The story of the Golem figure teaches a lesson of keeping a moral perspective in our undertakings. (T)

16. In the novel *The Sorrows of Werther,* young Werther kills his beloved Lotte because she has broken up with him. (F)

17. Plato claimed that art is harmful because it fans violent emotions. (T)

18. Aristotle viewed art as dangerous because it fans violent emotions. (F)

19. Karl Marx is famous for his little poignant short stories of political satire. (F)

20. Having a fictional friend is the same as having an imaginary friend. (F)

21. Baruch Spinoza said, "The wise man thinks about death continually." (F)

22. Aristotle claims that "Dramatic poetry has a most formidable power of corrupting even men of high character..." (F)

23. In Euripides's *The Bacchants* the young king Pentheus is killed by his mother, believing him to be a mountain lion. (T)

24. In *Pulp Fiction* Jules and Vincent have retrieved a briefcase full of jewelry from the gangster Wallace. (F)

Multiple-Choice Questions
(Correct answers are marked with an asterisk.)

25. The Trobriand people distinguish between three different kinds of stories. Which one does not belong on the list?
    a. sacred stories about the beginning of the world
    b. fairy tales told as entertainment
    c. semihistorical accounts of heroes
    *d. profane stories exaggerating one's personal achievements

26. The moral message of gruesome fairy tales may be the following:
    a. Evil is a continuous presence which we sooner or later fall victim to.
    b. Only evil people have evil things happen to them.
    c. Nothing is so bad that something good doesn't result from it.
    *d. Evil can be dealt with if we have fortitude.

27. What is a parable?
    a. the same as a fairy tale
    *b. an allegorical story for adults
    c. a concept from mathematics, describing a curve
    d. a story with two parallel endings

28. Why did the father of the prodigal son celebrate his homecoming?
    a. He had been away for thirty years.
    b. He brought his new wife with him.
    *c. The father had given him up for lost.
    d. The father was hoping that the son would help around the farm.

29. What is the implicit message of most slasher movies?
    *a. Sex and violent death are connected.
    b. Evil is always vanquished by the good.
    c. Violence is morally wrong, but sex is not.
    d. There is no implicit message in slasher movies.

30. What does Rosenstand mean by saying that we are temporal creatures?
    a. We are only on this earth for a short time, and then we are gone forever.
    b. We are endowed with temporal lobes.
    c. Most people have a hard time controlling their emotions; they are temperamental.
    *d. We are creatures who understand that we live in time; we remember the past and anticipate the future.

31. Chapter 2 mentions three key features connected to the act of telling one's own story. Which one shouldn't be on the list?
    a. The story is selective.
    b. The story is incomplete.
    c. The story is to some extent fictional.
    *d. The story is always true.

32. Who, in Chapter 2, speaks these words? "And I will strike down upon thee with great vengeance and furious anger those who attempt to poison and destroy my brothers..."
    *a. Jules, in *Pulp Fiction*
    b. Vincent, in *Pulp Fiction*
    c. Dionysus, in *The Bacchants*
    d. Werther, in *The Sorrows of Werther*

Essay/Study Questions

33. Relate the Trobriand myth of the grandmother who shed her skin, and analyze its moral message.

34. Relate the story of Abraham and Isaac, and analyze its meaning.

35. Compare Plato's and Aristotle's views on whether art has a positive or a negative influence, and discuss the topic of violence in films and on television with reference to Plato's and Aristotle's theories.

36. Discuss the following statement with examples from film and literature: "Literature can be used to raise one's awareness of potential future moral problems."

37. Discuss the mythologist Joseph Campbell's statement that one doesn't ask what one is doing at a party unless it is boring, meaning that one doesn't ask about the meaning of life unless one is unhappy.

38. How can telling our own story be not only a description of what we have done, but a prescription for what we think we ought to do in the future? Discuss. Try telling your own story as you might tell it to (1) a date, (2) a job interviewer, and (3) a journalist.

39. Do you agree with Plato that one ought always to be able to control one's emotions? Why or why not?

40. Evaluate the punishment given by Dionysus to Pentheus because he refused to accept the new religion. Is it fair treatment of the young king? Also, consider the punishment Agave, mother of Pentheus and a Dionysus follower herself, receives. Why do you think Euripides chose this plot?

41. What do you think is inside the suitcase in *Pulp Fiction*? Explain.

42. Evaluate the question of good and evil as it is presented in *Pulp Fiction*. What might Plato's reaction to this film be? Aristotle's?

CHAPTER 3
Ethical Relativism

True/False Questions

1. Some cultures feel that it is their moral duty to dispose of their seniors when they become unproductive. (T)

2. Hard universalism is the theory that we are each entitled to our own moral opinion and that there is no universal moral code. (F)

3. The moral nihilist believes that deep down all people have some values in common. (F)

4. King Darius found that the Callatians would not give up burning their dead, while the Greeks refused to give up eating their dead. (F)

5. Cultural relativism is a normative theory. (F)

6. Cultural relativism describes how customs differ from culture to culture. (T)

7. Ethical relativism is a normative theory. (T)

8. A normative ethical theory involves a moral judgment, evaluation, or justification. (T)

9. Benedict tells of the Northwest Coast Indians that when the chief's sister died, the tribe set out to find the culprits and kill them. (F)

10. Benedict's conclusion is that a certain behavior may be normal for a culture, but that doesn't mean it is morally right. (F)

11. Benedict is saying that morality is culturally defined. (T)

12. If a theory has a breaking point, it should be discarded altogether. (F)

13. Ethical relativism cannot make a claim to tolerance being universally good if all values are culture-relative. (T)

14. One of the arguments against ethical relativism says that the theory cannot distinguish between the actual morality and the professed morality of a culture. (T)

15. Because we can verify that the earth is round, we can also verify which moral viewpoints are better than others. (F)

16. The problem of induction is that induction induces people to think for themselves. (F)

17. One of the universal cultural values suggested by James Rachels is a rule against incest. (F)

18. Inclusive multiculturalism is also sometimes known as multicultural pluralism. (T)

19. Soft universalism claims there are some underlying values all cultures can agree on. (T)

20. In the primary readings, Benedict refers to a Melanesian culture that has developed paranoia into being the culturally accepted norm. (T)

21. Parekh argues in favor of monocultural education on the grounds that it facilitates cultural sensitivity. (F)

22. In Walker's narrative *Possessing the Secret of Joy,* the tribal practice of female circumcision is strongly condemned. (T)

23. In the narrative *A Passage to India,* Dr. Aziz is an Indian professor of philosophy. (F)

24. In *A Passage to India,* Adele withdraws all her accusations of assault. (T)

25. In the film *Do The Right Thing,* Mookie's life is saved by a black police officer. (F)

26. In *Do The Right Thing,* the Korean store owner claims to be black. (T)

Multiple-Choice Questions
(Correct answers are marked with an asterisk.)

27. One of these answers is not on the list of the four major approaches to the phenomenon of moral differences:
    a. hard universalism.
    b. ethical relativism.
    *c. ethical egoism.
    d. soft universalism.

28. Why is the problem of induction a problem for ethical relativism?
    a. because it induces people to think for themselves
    *b. because we can never know for certain when we have accumulated enough material to make a theory
    c. because we should be using the method of *deduction,* not induction
    d. because very few people understand the problem of induction

29. What is the key issue for Benedict?
    a. Normality is culturally defined.
    b. The concept of the normal is a variant of the concept of the good.
    c. The majority of any group conform to the values of the group; the deviants are few.
    *d. all of the above

30. Which one of these four arguments is not one of the main arguments against ethical relativism?
    a. Ethical relativism forces us to bow to majority rule.
    b. We can neither condemn nor praise other cultures.
    c. It is hard to determine what might constitute a morally autonomous subgroup.
    *d. Ethical relativism is blasphemous, so it should be prohibited.

31. According to Rachels, there are three universal moral standards, disproving ethical relativism. Which one of these doesn't belong on the list?
    a.   a prohibition against lying
    b.   care of enough infants to keep society going
    *c. a prohibition against incest
    d.   a prohibition against murder

32. What is an *ad hominem* argument?
    *a. a logical fallacy claiming that you are right or wrong because of who you are, not because of what you say
    b.   a logical fallacy claiming that if *A = B*, then *B = A*
    c.   an argument that is valid for only one particular set of circumstances
    d.   an argument devised by men, for men, to the exclusion of women

33. Who expresses the following claim? "Mankind has always preferred to say, 'It is a morally good,' rather than 'It is habitual'... But historically the two phrases are synonymous."
    a.   James Rachels
    *b. Ruth Benedict
    c.   Alice Walker
    d.   Bhikhu Parekh

34. Bhikhu Parekh lists five evil consequences of monocultural education. Out of these four, which one should not be on the list?
    a.   Monocultural education is unlikely to awaken the student's faculty of imagination.
    b.   Monocultural education stunts the growth of the critical faculty.
    c.   Monocultural education encourages arrogance and insensitivity.
    *d. Monocultural education stunts the growth of self-alienation.

35. What is the culturally sensitive topic of Alice Walker's *Possessing the Secret of Joy*?
    a.   female infanticide
    b.   male circumcision
    *c. female circumcision
    d.   euthanasia

36. In the film *Do The Right Thing* a riot begins. What is the immediate cause of the riot?
    *a. Radio Raheem is killed by the police.
    b.   Mookie is killed by the police.
    c.   Sal kills Radio Raheem.
    d.   De Mayor throws a trash can at Sal's pizzeria.

Essay/Study Questions

37. Outline the four major approaches to moral phenomena that Rosenstand sketches on pp. 76–77. Which one best illustrates your own position?

38. Why would hard universalism (moral absolutism) be the attitude most often supported by ethical theories and everyday experience? What does this position say about the nature of ethics as a theoretical or reflective endeavor? Why might one prefer the consistency and universalism of this position?

39. Clarify the differences between descriptive and normative ethics. Can we always separate the activity of description and normative judgment?

40. Describe the theory of ethical relativism, and illustrate it with an example from the text.

41. Relate the story of King Darius, the Greeks, and the Callatians, and discuss its implications.

42. What kind of claim is Ruth Benedict making when she claims that there are no universal moral standards? What does it mean to say that "[we] have no right to claim that our choice is better than any other culture's" (p. 69)?

43. Explore the consequences of the argument that we can neither condemn nor praise other cultures. Do you agree? Why or why not?

44. If we accept relativism, why must we "bow to majority rule"? Should we assume that the position of power will flow out of a democratic, numerical majority? What was the case in South Africa until recent political memory?

45. What is the problem between the professed morality and actual morality when it comes to assessing "normality" in a community according to the theory of ethical relativism? If moral norms are subjective between communities, how do specific communities enforce their norms upon their individual members?

46. Explain the problem of induction as it relates to the debate about moral norms.

47. What are the three values that James Rachels considers universal? Can you think of any others?

48. Compare exclusive multiculturalism with inclusive multiculturalism, and discuss the implications of both forms.

49. Discuss the five consequences of monocultural education outlined by Parekh: Is he right? Why or why not? Does Parekh advocate inclusive or exclusive multiculturalism?

50. In Walker's *Possessing the Secret of Joy,* Tashi's husband Adam asks, "Why is the child crying?" What does he mean by that?

CHAPTER 4
Myself or Others?

True/False Questions

1. An egoist is a person who, by definition, thinks highly of himself or herself and utilizes self-praise consistently. (F)

2. A psychological egoist is by definition a selfish person. (F)

3. A psychological egoist is a person who believes that everyone is selfish. (T)

4. "Ought implies can" usually means the same as "if there is a will there is a way." (F)

5. Glaucon uses the story of the Ring of Gyges to express his moral disapproval of anyone who gains an advantage by disregarding the interests of others. (F)

6. The story of the Ring of Gyges indicates that humans will take advantage of any situation if they can get away with it. (T)

7. Psychological egoism is the theory that the only proper way to live is to be selfish; in other words, everyone isn't necessarily selfish by nature, but one ought to be selfish. (F)

8. Glaucon claims that if we gave away two invisibility rings, one to a just person and one to an unjust person, the unjust person would take advantage of the ring, but the just person would not. (F)

9. Thomas Hobbes thought that all acts, even acts of pity, could be attributed to a natural tendency toward selfishness. (T)

10. Inuit whale hunters helped free the whales trapped in the ice off the coast of Alaska. (T)

11. Hedonism means pleasure-seeking. (T)

12. A theory must be theoretically falsifiable in order to be philosophically acceptable. (T)

13. If a theory cannot be falsified under any circumstances, it must be true. (F)

14. Abraham Lincoln was a psychological egoist. (T)

15. The fallacy of the suppressed correlative is a way to refute psychological egoism through logic. (T)

16. Ethical egoism is a decent way to be selfish. (F)

17. An ethical egoist is a person believing that everybody is selfish. (F)

18. Individual ethical egoism is the theory that everyone ought to do what I want. (T)

19. Ethical egoism is a consequentialist theory. (T)

20. The word *altruism* means the same as the word *hedonism*. (F)

21. David Hume believes that all humans are selfish at heart. (F)

22. David Hume holds the theory that humans are by nature benevolent. (T)

23. Peter Singer claims that it is to everyone's evolutionary advantage to look after their own interests and disregard the interests of others. (F)

24. Reciprocal altruism is known as Golden Rule Altruism. (T)

25. Psychological altruism claims that everyone is unselfish by nature. (T)

26. It has been proven to the satisfaction of most scientists that chimpanzees have no trace of moral rules in their society. (F)

27. Ayn Rand claims that it is acceptable, for selfish reasons, to save a drowning person under certain circumstances. (T)

28. In the film *Hero*, Bernie takes the credit for saving crew and passengers aboard a burning plane, while the true savior of the flight was a homeless person, John Bubber. (F)

29. Emma Bovary persuades her husband to let her take piano lessons because she really wants an excuse to go to town, so she can meet with her illegitimate daughter. (F)

30. *Atlas Shrugged* can be seen as an argument for accepting altruism as the only acceptable ethical theory. (F)

Multiple-Choice Questions
(Correct answers are marked with an asterisk.)

31. Psychological egoism claims that:
    a. most people will act selfishly if they think they can get away with it.
    b. people always ought to act selfishly.
    c. egoists have a psychological problem.
    *d. people always act selfishly.

32. What is Glaucon's point with his hypothesis of the two rings in the text by Plato?
    a. that any man who has two rings ought to give one of them to a needy person
    b. that if we have two invisibility rings and give one to a good man and one to a bad one, the good man will do good deeds with it and the bad man will do bad deeds
    c. that if we have two invisibility rings and give one to a good man and one to a bad one, the good man will do bad deeds and the bad man will do good deeds
    *d. that if we have two invisibility rings and give one to a good man and one to a bad one, the good man and the bad man will both behave selfishly

33. Why do we feel pity toward others, according to Thomas Hobbes?
    a. We are benevolent by nature and feel sympathetic toward others.
    *b. We are afraid their misfortune might happen to us.
    c. We are afraid they will find out that we don't care about their misfortune.
    d. We are stupid. Smart people don't feel pity, according to Hobbes.

34. There are three major reasons for choosing to believe in psychological egoism.
    a. the theory appeals to our modern-day cynicism
    b. the theory appeals to our honesty
    *c. the theory allows us to choose when to be selfish and when to consider the feelings of others
    d. the theory serves as an excuse for not trying to do something for others

35. What is the paradox of hedonism?
    a. You can never have too much pleasure.
    b. You cannot love more than one person at the same time.
    c. You must find pleasure in your own company before you can find pleasure in the company of others.
    *d. The harder you look for pleasure, the more it is likely to elude you.

36. What is the fallacy of the suppressed correlative?
    a. the same as an *ad hominem* argument
    b. to believe that you can understand yourself by suppressing your memories of your family history
    *c. one way of criticizing psychological egoism: it suppresses the term of unselfishness, which is the correlative of selfishness
    d. to think you can avoid a problem by suppressing it

37. Three major criticisms against psychological egoism are listed in the textbook. Which one should not be on the list?
    a. Falsification is not possible, because psychological egoism doesn't allow for the possibility that some people are not selfish all the time.
    b. The theory has problems with the language it uses, including the fallacy of the suppressed correlative.
    c. The theory mistakenly assumes that doing what we want is always selfish.
    *d. The theory misinterprets the old saying, "Ought implies can," to mean "If I ought to do something, then I will be able to do it."

38. Abraham Lincoln claimed that he saved the pigs from drowning because
    *a. he wouldn't have had peace of mind all day otherwise.
    b. they were his property, and he didn't want to lose the investment.
    c. he wanted to prove that he was a good and kind person.
    d. he liked pigs.

39. Ethical egoism doesn't work in practice because
    a. some people are not willing to be selfish.
    *b. if everybody looks after his or her own self-interests, then you will have a lot of competition.
    c. humans are by nature benevolent.
    d. if you try to look after your own interests, you will be hindered by others who disapprove of ethical egoism.

40. In the primary reading, Ayn Rand lists four implications of accepting altruism. Which one shouldn't be on the list?
    a. a lack of self-esteem
    b. a hopelessly cynical amorality
    *c. a lack of cultural sensitivity
    d. a lack of respect for others

41. Why did Emma Bovary take her own life?
    a. Because she was terminally ill.
    b. Because her lover had left her.
    *c. Because she had sold all her own and her husband's assets to pay off her debt.
    d. Because her daughter had found out that she had been seeing another man and threatened to tell Charles Bovary.

42. In *Atlas Shrugged,* Ayn Rand's main concern is:
    a. to make people understand that it is everyone's responsibility to make certain that no one goes hungry in this world.
    b. to make people understand ethical relativism.
    *c. to make people understand that it is everyone's right to protect himself or herself from being used by others who want something for nothing.
    d. to make people understand that the Bible is always right.

Essay/Study Questions

43. What is the difference between psychological egoism and ethical egoism?

44. Consider the story of the passerby at the Potomac River. Explain his behavior in terms of psychological egoism. Is this explanation adequate? If not, why not?

45. Do you agree with Rosenstand that cynicism may account for some of the popularity of psychological egoism? Why or why not?

46. Consider the "ought implies can" section on p. 84. How do psychological egoists defend that human selfishness is a matter of "fact"?

47. Give a brief account of the story of the Ring of Gyges. How does Glaucon use it to express a hypothesis of human nature?

48. What are the three arguments that Hobbes gives to support the legitimacy of the social contract?

49. How does Hobbes account for human pity? Can you raise any counter-examples to his arguments?

50. What is hedonism and what are some of the problems associated with it as a moral theory?

51. Would you characterize Lincoln's opinion of his own act of saving the pigs as that of a psychological or an ethical egoist? Your answer should contain a precise definition of both theories.

52. What is the "fallacy of the suppressed correlative"? Use an example to explain. Try to think of an application of the fallacy that is not mentioned in the text.

53. Explain why ethical egoism is not a valid moral theory.

54. What are some of the problems associated with the life of an ethical egoist?

55. Give an account of Singer's argument against ethical egoism.

56. What is the difference between ideal and reciprocal altruism? Explain.

57. Why does Rosenstand claim that moral theories must be extended to everyone (p. 97)?

58. When, according to Ayn Rand, would it be morally acceptable to save a drowning person? Explain and add your own comments.

59. Evaluate the moral message of *Hero,* and relate it to the theories of psychological egoism, ethical egoism, and ideal and limited altruism.

CHAPTER 5
Using Your Reason, Part 1: Utilitarianism

True/False Questions

1. The principle of utility is the same as the greatest happiness principle. (T)

2. Any theory concerned with the consequences of actions is a utilitarian theory. (F)

3. For Bentham, moral goodness is the same as pleasure, and moral evil is the same as pain. (T)

4. Bentham's interest in moral theory was primarily theoretical. (F)

5. An instrumental value is something you value for its own sake. (F)

6. One reason Bentham donated his body to science was to put a stop to body-snatching. (T)

7. Bentham believes that pleasure is an intrinsic value. (T)

8. A value cannot be both intrinsic and instrumental at the same time. (F)

9. The hedonistic calculus is a method by which we calculate the utility of an action according to its ability to produce pleasure or prevent pain. (T)

10. The hedonistic calculus is a method designed primarily to calculate how much pain and pleasure you yourself will get out of a course of action. (F)

11. One of the arguments against the hedonistic calculus is that it promotes selfish interests. (F)

12. One of the arguments against the hedonistic calculus is that it is biased in favor of our choice of values. (T)

13. Descartes argued that animals can't feel pain, because they have no mind. (T)

14. Even though Descartes never owned a pet, he was sensitive to the suffering of animals. (F)

15. Mill claims that utilitarianism fails, because we can never make a decision since we cannot calculate all future consequences. (F)

16. For Bentham the criterion for who belongs in the moral universe is who can suffer. (T)

17. Utilitarianism is against any form of animal experiments because experiments cause suffering to the animal. (F)

18. Utilitarianism might allow for using human suffering as a means of entertainment if the happiness produced outweighs the suffering. (T)

19. J. S. Mill claims that it is better to be a pig than to be a fool. (F)

20. The philosopher Epicurus was J. S. Mill's godfather. (F)

21. Mill claims that something is desirable if it is desired. (T)

22. The naturalistic fallacy attempts to make a statement about what is the case based on a statement about what ought to be the case. (F)

23. Mill believed that the government should not interfere with people's lives unless they do harm to themselves. (F)

24. Mill was a champion of women's rights. (T)

25. Mill believed that whole populations could not be trusted to govern themselves because they were not sufficiently mature. (T)

26. Act and rule utilitarianism are one and the same thing. (F)

27. In the primary readings, Bentham declares the interest of the community to be of less importance than the interest of the individual. (F)

28. In the primary readings, Mill claims that happiness is the same as contentment. (F)

29. In the primary reading, Mill insists that next to selfishness, the principal cause which makes life unsatisfactory is want of mental cultivation. (T)

30.' In "The Blacksmith and the Baker," an innocent baker is being executed for the crime of the blacksmith. (T)

31. In *The Brothers Karamazov,* Alyosha would not consent to the torture of a small creature for the sake of human happiness. (T)

32. In "The Ones Who Walk Away from Omelas," the happiness of the community is based on a dog being tortured. (F)

33. In *Outbreak,* the president's aide points out that the firebombing of Cedar Creek to save the rest of the nation is, in fact, constitutional. (F)

Multiple-Choice Questions
(Correct answers are marked with an asterisk.)

34. Utilitarianism would agree to which one of the following statements?
    a. It is morally praiseworthy to disregard one's own interests for the sake of other people.
    *b. The end justifies the means.
    c. God determines the ultimate values of good and evil.
    d. Might makes right.

35. Mill disagrees with Bentham by claiming the following:
    a. The principle of utility is the one universal moral principle.
    b. The greatest happiness principle is the one universal moral principle.
    *c. There is a qualitative difference between pleasures.
    d. There is a quantitative difference between pleasures.

36. Utilitarianism may agree to animal experiments under certain circumstances. Which is the most likely circumstance?
    a. any time, because we have no obligations to nonrational creatures
    *b. whenever it is likely to bring about so much happiness or decrease unhappiness to such a degree that it outweighs the suffering of the animal
    c. whenever we can determine that the suffering of the animal is minimal
    d. whenever there is a large amount of happiness at stake in terms of profit for the doctors, the university, or business

37. How does Mill propose to determine which pleasures are higher and which are lower?
    a. by taking a poll in a local region
    b. by selecting answers from people capable of appreciating higher pleasures and having no experience with lower pleasures
    *c. by asking people who have experience with both kinds of pleasure
    d. by reading the newspapers

38. Who wrote, "Capacity for the nobler feeling is in most natures a very tender plant, easily killed, not only by hostile influences, but by mere want of sustenance"?
    a. Bentham
    b. Epicurus
    c. Benedict
    *d. Mill

39. According to J. S. Mill, there is only one legitimate reason for interfering with other people's lives:
    *a. if they do harm to others.
    b. if they do harm to themselves.
    c. if you possess relevant knowledge about their welfare that is unavailable to them.
    d. Trick question: Mill thought there were NO legitimate reasons to interfere with other people's lives.

40. What is act utilitarianism?
    a. the same as rule utilitarianism: the consequences of any type of act (rule) are what count
    *b. the same as Bentham's utilitarianism: the consequences of any single act are what count
    c. the opposite of passive utilitarianism
    d. the part of utilitarianism that allows you to think of yourself only

41. One of these statements is by John Stuart Mill. Which one?
    a. "The proper method of judging when or whether one should help another person is by reference to one's own rational self-interest and one's own hierarchy of values."
    b. "No one civilization can possibly utilize in its mores the whole potential range of human behavior."
    *c. "A being of higher faculties requires more to make him happy, is capable probably of more acute suffering, and certainly accessible to it at more points, than one of an inferior type."
    d. "The question is not, Can they speak, nor Can they reason, but Can they suffer?"

42. In "The Blacksmith and the Baker" the judge pronounces a sentence. What is his justification?
    a. The baker is guilty and must be punished.
    b. The townspeople have bribed him to let the blacksmith go.
    c. The blacksmith must be punished for his crime, and nobody can take his place.
    *d. The baker can be punished even if he is innocent, because he is expendable, but the blacksmith is not.

43. In *The Brothers Karamazov*, Ivan tells Alyosha about an incident involving a small child: Which one is it?
    a. The child is kept in a basement so that the city may prosper.
    *b. The child is torn apart by dogs on the order of a general.
    c. The child is accused of murdering Ivan's father.
    d. The child is saved from drowning by the dogs belonging to a general.

44. In *Outbreak* the key issue is:
    a. whether it is justifiable to keep a child in perpetual suffering for the sake of general happiness.
    b. whether a mother should sacrifice herself for her children.
    *c. whether it is justifiable to annihilate a community to preserve the lives of millions.
    d. whether leaking news to the press is ethical.

Essay/Study Questions

45. The opening sentence of this chapter refers to the role "reason or instinct" might play in the formation of a moral guideline that seeks the good of a majority. What are some of the differences between reason and instinct?

46. What is the difference between intrinsic and instrumental reasoning? Give an example.

47. What is Bentham's "hedonistic calculus"? What might this device tell us about the Age of Reason and the type of arguments that would be considered important in such an age? Give an example of how to use the calculus.

48. Why does Bentham refuse to distinguish between choices, between going to the opera and drinking gin? What would John Stuart Mill make of this example?

49. What were some of the points of Bentham's moral theory that J. S. Mill reconsidered in his formulation of utilitarianism?

50. According to Mill, how can we make a decision without knowing the consequences? Explain and discuss.

51. What is the harm principle? Explain with an example.

52. Explain the difference between act utilitarianism and rule utilitarianism.

53. Explain the general idea of the naturalistic fallacy and how it relates to utilitarianism.

54. Using Aristotle's claim that "man by nature desires to know," how would you explain Mill's political vision of providing everyone the opportunity of enjoying opera and other "higher" pursuits?

55. What constitutes (and what does not constitute) "harm" for Mill? How might this relate to the debate about freedom of speech?

56. How would a utilitarian respond to the suggestion that alien beings would be allowed to abduct involuntary human subjects for lethal medical experiments provided that they give humanity a cure for all viral diseases, including AIDS? Evaluate the answer from the standpoint of an act utilitarian and a rule utilitarian.

57. Evaluate the following statement from a utilitarian point of view: "Tests are causing suffering to students, and professors always complain about having to grade tests, so tests should be abolished."

58. Evaluate Descartes's theory that only those beings with minds can suffer, and only human beings have minds. Explore the possible consequences for a moral theory if we agree that animals, including human beings, have the capacity for suffering.

59. Do you agree with Mill that "A being of higher faculties requires more to make him happy...than one of an inferior type"? What does Mill mean by "inferior"?

60. If you were a citizen of Omelas, and were shown the child in captivity, would you stay and accept the lesson about the price of happiness, or would you walk away from Omelas? Explain.

CHAPTER 6
Using Your Reason, Part 2: Kant's Deontology

True/False Questions

1. In Kant's moral theory, we use our maxim primarily to maximize the happiness of everyone involved. (F)

2. In Kant's view, a good will cannot be good if it doesn't take consequences of one's actions into account. (F)

3. In Kant's view, a good will is good regardless of whether it accomplishes its purpose or not. (T)

4. Kant is a hard universalist. (T)

5. The hypothetical imperative is a conditional command, describing an "if-then" situation. (T)

6. According to Kant, an act that is done for other reasons than a sense of duty is not necessarily a morally wrong act. (T)

7. A maxim is an act that has a maximum amount of good consequences. (F)

8. Universalization means to ask yourself if everyone actually agrees with your own moral values. (F)

9. When we universalize a maxim, we ask ourselves if it could be made into a universal law. (T)

10. To be an autonomous lawmaker means that you are a member of the government and you cannot be bribed. (F)

11. Kant has been criticized for claiming that his theory does not take consequences into account, when in fact it does. (T)

12. Among the criticisms raised against Kant's categorical imperative is the following: The categorical imperative discriminates against people of no or low income. (F)

13. According to Kant, a rational being is any being capable of feeling pleasure or pain. (F)

14. Being used as merely a means to an end is the same as being regarded as having instrumental value only. (T)

15. Being treated as a means to an end is the same as being used merely as a means. (F)

16. Rational beings have intrinsic value according to Kant. (T)

17. Rebecca, a college student, is being used merely as a means to an end by her college professors because they get paid for teaching classes, and without Rebecca and other students they would not receive a paycheck. (F)

18. Kant thinks that we may treat animals any way we like, including being cruel to them. (F)

19. Humans who don't qualify as rational beings must, according to Kant's own theory, be classified as things. (T)

20. According to Kant, humans have free choice; animal choice is merely brutish. (T)

21. Kanzi, the bonobo chimpanzee, is famous for being the first ape to master basic human speech with his own vocal cords. (F)

22. Kanzi, the bonobo chimpanzee, is famous for communicating with humans using a lexigram. (T)

23. "Kingdom of Ends" refers to Kant's theory of history: When everyone has learned to use the categorical imperative, history will come to an end. (F)

24. Kant was against animal experimentation for the sake of mere speculation. (T)

25. For Kant, lying (in the ethical sense) must be shown to be harmful to others in order to be considered morally wrong. (F)

26. In *Abandon Ship!*, Captain Holmes is concerned primarily with saving his own life. (F)

27. In *Rebel Without a Cause,* Jim challenges the local gang leader to a "chickie-run." (F)

28. In *Star Trek: The Next Generation,* "Justice," Wesley is about to be executed for trespassing. (T)

29. In *The Bridges of Madison County,* Francesca ruins the lives of her family by eloping with the love of her life, Robert Kinckaid, and lives to regret it. (F)

Multiple-Choice Questions
(Correct answers are marked with an asterisk.)

30. What is a deontological theory?
    a. a theory about proper dental care
    b. a theory assessing the overall consequences of an action
    c. the same as a consequentialist theory
    *d. a theory assessing the morality of an action in terms of duty or rightness in itself

31. A store owner is trying to decide whether or not to cheat her customers. Which one of her arguments would qualify as a moral decision, according to Kant?
    a. She decides to try to cheat her customers on occasion when she is certain she can get away with it.
    b. She decides not to cheat her customers because it would not be prudent: She might be found out and lose all her customers.

*c. She decides not to cheat her customers because such an act could not be made into a universal law.

d. She decides not to cheat her customers because she likes them very much.

32. What is an autonomous lawmaker?
    a. a member of the government who cannot be bribed
    b. someone who is capable of influencing the legislation in his or her own favor
    *c. a person who follows the categorical imperative
    d. a person who follows hypothetical imperatives

33. Which one of the following is not a major criticism raised against Kant's moral theory?
    *a. The categorical imperative discriminates against people of no or low income.
    b. There is a loophole in the categorical imperative: A situation can be described so specifically that it doesn't apply.
    c. The categorical imperative doesn't allow for exceptions.
    d. The view of what is rational depends on who holds the view.

34. Kant has three main themes in his book *Grounding*. Which one of the following does not belong?
    a. the theory that people should be treated as ends in themselves
    *b. the theory about the inalienable right to the pursuit of happiness for rational beings
    c. the theory of the categorical imperative
    d. the theory of people forming a moral community, the Kingdom of Ends

35. What does Kant mean by "universal law"?
    a. a law of physics, like gravity
    b. a moral law dictated by a moral authority
    *c. a moral law, binding for all rational beings
    d. a civic law, binding for all citizens

36. What does Kant mean by "the right to a person akin to a thing?"
    a. a defense of the right to own slaves
    b. a defense of property rights
    *c. an intermediate category of being a person, but without complete freedom
    d. an intermediate category of being half saint, half devil

37. What, according to Kant, is an internal lie?
    *a. a lie that someone tells himself or herself
    b. a lie that has harmful results to the liar only
    c. a mistake
    d. a lie that causes no harm, but actually brings benefits to all involved

38. In the film *Abandon Ship!*, Captain Holmes put several survivors over the side of the lifeboat. Why?
    a.   He was afraid they would gang up on him and kill him.
    *b. He was trying to save the lives of the strongest survivors.
    c.   He was trying to save the lives of the weakest survivors.
    d.   He was mainly trying to save his own life.

39. In *Rebel Without a Cause,* Jim's father tries to give him advice. Which one of the following theories does his father seem to subscribe to?
    a.   a Kantian deontological theory
    b.   a theory of psychological egoism
    c.   a theory of ethical relativism
    *d. a theory of utilitarianism

40. In *Star Trek: The Next Generation,* "Justice," Picard stops Wesley's execution by presenting an argument that is acceptable to the planet's rulers. What is the argument?
    a.   Wesley is underage and can't be held responsible.
    b.   Nobody can be held responsible for not knowing the laws of a foreign culture.
    *c. A moral law is not mature if it does not allow for exceptions.
    d.   A moral law of one culture should not be binding on members of another culture.

41. In *The Bridges of Madison County,* Francesca agonizes over whether to leave her family for her lover. Which one of these is the argument that finally persuades her?
    a.   She must go with Robert, because such certainly of love comes but once in a lifetime.
    b.   She will be punished by eternal damnation if she leaves her family.
    c.   She realizes that not only will her family suffer, but the entire community will suffer if she leaves.
    *d. She realizes that her children will suffer, and that her daughter would get the wrong message about love and relationships if she leaves.

Essay/Study Questions

42. What is "universalization"? Explain, and give an example.

43. What is a hypothetical imperative? Explain in detail, and give an example.

44. What is the categorical imperative? Give an example. Why should someone obey the dictates of the categorical imperative?

45. What is the difference between the ideal situation and the actual situation in assessing the universalizability of the categorical imperative?

46. What are some problems with the categorical imperative? Why has it nevertheless been so influential in ethical theory?

47. Evaluate the following statement: "Actions are only morally good if they are done because of a good will." Explain "good will," and give reasons why you think the statement is correct or incorrect.

48. Analyze the following statement: "Act in such a way that you treat humanity, whether in your own person or in the person of another, always at the same time as an end and never simply as a means."

49. What does it mean to treat someone as "an end in himself or herself," rather than a means (only)?

50. What is Kant's criterion of rationality for the recognition of personhood? What (or who) does it leave out?

51. Discuss the case of Kanzi, the chimpanzee who communicates with the help of a lexigram. Would Kant accept him as an end in himself? Why or why not? Would you?

52. What is the Kingdom of Ends?

CHAPTER 7
Personhood, Rights, and Justice

True/False Questions

1. A human being is always identified as a person. (F)

2. Kant claims that you qualify as a person if you are a rational being. (T)

3. Kant claims that any being capable of suffering qualifies for personhood. (F)

4. *Patria potestas* is the right of the father to treat his family any way he pleases. (T)

5. Kant's theory of personhood might include nonhuman beings who are rational. (T)

6. Many social thinkers prefer using the term *person* instead of *human being*. (T)

7. Historically, gods and goddesses, totems, and dead ancestors have been granted personhood. (T)

8. Saint Augustine specified that the soul is not present in the fetus until it is capable of feeling. (T)

9. A *homunculus* means a tiny person; in the textbook we meet the concept in the old conviction that inside each person's head is a small copy of that person, representing the soul. (F)

10. Judith Jarvis Thomson proposes an analogy to the abortion question: If you found yourself in a hospital bed, attached to a famous violinist, you'd have no right to unplug yourself. (F)

11. A pro-choice utilitarian will use the rights of the woman as a key argument. (F)

12. A pro-choice deontologist will use the rights of the woman as a key argument. (T)

13. In earlier times, animals were put on trial for crimes. (T)

14. John Stuart Mill argued in favor of universal right to self-determination, provided that the individuals in question have been properly educated. (T)

15. Jeremy Bentham was critical of the concept of rights. (T)

16. Ronald Dworkin is in favor of what he calls the first model: We have to find a balance between the rights of the individual and the demands of society. (F)

17. A negative right is a right not to be interfered with. (T)

18. A negative right is a right that a society disapproves of. (F)

19. The three negative rights advocated by John Locke are: The right to life, liberty, and the pursuit of happiness. (F)

20. Ayn Rand agrees with John Locke about the three negative rights. (T)

21. John Hospers and Ayn Rand both express views that are shared by many libertarians. (T)

22. A positive right is the same as an entitlement. (T)

23. When we apply the veil of ignorance, we find ourselves in the original position, according to John Rawls. (T)

24. The *original position* theory is a modern version of the old social contract theory. (T)

25. Elizabeth Wolgast argues that since humans are social atoms, the original position is an ingenious practical aid in determining social fairness. (F)

26. Elizabeth Wolgast is an advocate of communitarianism. (T)

27. Marilyn Friedman argues that community traditions may often be oppressive to women. (T)

28. Utilitarianism may conclude that those patients with a higher quality of life should have preferential treatment to those patients with a lower quality of life. (T)

29. Peter Kemp is an advocate of the idea that since everyone is irreplaceable, everyone should be respected as a person and not as a commodity. (T)

30. A modern philosophical theory of rights says that if you are capable of having interests, then you should have rights. (T)

31. Suggested rights for the great apes involve the right not to be killed, the right not to be deprived of their freedom, and the right not to have their environment destroyed. (F)

32. According to the theory of interests, if you are a being capable of suffering, and you have an interest, then you have a right to have that interest met. (F)

33. Steve Sapontzis argues from both a utilitarian and a Kantian viewpoint in favor of animal rights. (T)

34. Distributive justice: The justice meted out to a person who has broken the law. (F)

35. Retribution is a backward-looking reason for punishment. (T)

36. Deterrence is a backward-looking theory of punishment. (F)

37. A retentionist can be a retributivist, but can also be a utilitarian. (T)

38. Article 3 in the Declaration of Human Rights states that "everyone has a right to life, liberty, and property." (F)

39. In the Declaration of Human Rights there are examples of both positive and negative rights. (T)

40. For Rawls, it is acceptable to allow an inequality as long as only a small minority of the population suffer because of it. (F)

41. The *Blade Runner* replicants are all unaware that they are artificial beings. (F)

42. In "The Jigsaw Man," Lew is in prison, awaiting trial for organlegging. (F)

Multiple-Choice Questions
(Correct answers are marked with an asterisk.)

43. What does the term "homunculus" stand for?
    *a. It means a tiny person.
    b. It is a social term for children being raised by their mother's brother.
    c. It is a philosophical term meaning personhood.
    d. It is an older term for "humongous."

44. Mary Ann Warren lists five criteria for personhood. Identify the one that should not be on the list.
    a. consciousness and the ability to feel pain
    b. capacity for reason
    *c. emotional bonding with other beings of its own kind
    d. self-awareness

45. Who makes the following claim? "Invading a right is far worse than inflating it."
    a. Ayn Rand
    *b. Ronald Dworkin
    c. John Rawls
    d. Marilyn Friedman

46. In libertarian philosophy three negative rights are emphasized. Which one shouldn't be on the list?
    a. the right to liberty
    b. the right to life
    *c. the pursuit of happiness
    d. the right to property

47. Three thinkers mentioned in the textbook agree about the three negative rights. Which one shouldn't be on the list?
    a. Ayn Rand
    *b. John Rawls
    c. John Locke
    d. John Hospers

48. Who says, "There is only one fundamental right: the right to your on life, and to act free of coercion"?
    a. John Rawls
    b. Jeremy Bentham
    *c. Ayn Rand
    d. Ronald Dworkin

49. Which description best characterizes the *original position*?
    a. the first premise in any argument
    b. the fetal position
    c. the famous concept of "workfare not welfare"
    *d. a principle for fair distribution: make rules as if you didn't know who you might be when they take effect

50. Who is the author of the following statement? "We need to loosen the hold that the atomistic model has on our thinking, and recognize the importance that theory has on our judgments and our moral condition."
    a. John Rawls
    b. Ayn Rand
    c. Marilyn Friedman
    *d. Elizabeth Wolgast

51. Which philosopher would be most likely to associate rights with duties and responsibilities?
    *a. Kant
    b. Bentham
    c. Singer
    d. Feinberg

52. There are five common approaches to punishment. Out of these four, select the one that is not considered legitimate by legal experts.
    a. rehabilitation
    *b. vengeance
    c. retribution
    d. deterrence

53. There are three factors separating retribution from vengeance. Which one shouldn't be on the list?
    a. Retribution is based on logic, while vengeance is an emotional response.
    *b. Retribution is forward-looking, while vengeance is backward-looking.
    c. Retribution wants punishment to fit the crime, while vengeance may exceed the damage done by the criminal.
    d. Retribution is a public act, while vengeance is a private enterprise.

54. Which of these approaches cannot support retentionism?
    *a. rehabilitation
    b. incapacitation
    c. deterrence
    d. retribution

55. What is the most important moral question asked in *Blade Runner*?
    *a. Is it right to create a race of artificial humans without giving them human rights?
    b. Is bounty hunting morally acceptable?
    c. Is it right for a detective to become emotionally involved with his or her client?
    d. Is it right to create artificial animals without any concern for the environment?

56. "The Jigsaw Man" can be read as a criticism of what?
    a. backward-looking theories of punishment
    *b. forward-looking theories of punishment
    c. animal rights
    d. the Kantian concept of personhood

Essay/Study Questions

57. Discuss the issue of whether or not the fetus is a person, explaining your criteria for personhood. Now explain whether or not the idea of fetal personhood ought to be relevant for the abortion issue.

58. What, to you, is a person? Is it necessarily the same as a human being? Explain. Is it conceivable that a person might not be human?

59. Why does Bentham say that rights are "nonsense upon stilts"? Evaluate his statement.

60. Discuss Dworkin's two models, and identify his own viewpoint. Do you agree with him? Why or why not?

61. Discuss the issue of rights and responsibilities: Is it acceptable to link rights with responsibilities? Why or why not?

62. Discuss the three negative rights, and identify the philosophers who advocate them. Outline some of the social and political consequences of enforcing these rights. Do you agree to such consequences? Why or why not?

63. Identify the three human rights advocated by the libertarians, and explain briefly (your answer should contain a definition of negative rights and positive rights).

64. What is a thought experiment? How can Rawls's "original position" be called a thought experiment? What are the social advantages of this position? Can you think of any disadvantages?

65. Explain the view that if a being can suffer, then it has interests, and if it has interests, then they should be taken into consideration. Apply this to the issue of rights for the great apes, and discuss whether the suggestion of rights for the nonhuman great apes has merit.

66. What is meant by distributive justice? What is meant by criminal justice? Explain the difference.

67. Define retentionism and abolitionism, and relate these approaches to the five reasons for punishment. Do you personally think the death penalty should be retained or abolished? Why or why not? Explain.

68. Read the Declaration of Human Rights, and evaluate the articles from (1) a libertarian approach and (2) from Rawls's approach.

69. Evaluate Article 11 from (1) a utilitarian and (2) a Kantian approach.

70. Describe Rawls's two principles in your own words, and discuss them. Are there advantages, as you see it? Are there disadvantages?

71. How might Kant have reacted to the moral question raised in *Blade Runner*? How might Bentham have reacted? Identify the moral question, formulate Kant's and Bentham's answers, and discuss them.

72. Should we take Niven's story about "The Jigsaw Man" seriously? Why or why not?

CHAPTER 8
Socrates, Plato, and the Good Life

True/False Questions

1. Virtue-ethics is commonly opposed to ethics of character. (F)

2. Hypatia was a woman philosopher in Egypt. (T)

3. Hypatia was murdered by a mob of fanatical Christian monks. (T)

4. Socrates reportedly claimed that "an unlived life is not worth examining." (F)

5. The Socratic method is also known as a dialectic method. (T)

6. Socrates was primarily interested in teaching the sons and daughters of the Athenian working population. (F)

7. Socrates implied that he was not bound to any one conception of reality unless it could be tested by reason. (T)

8. Socrates was executed by beheading on the final day of the Olympic games. (F)

9. Crito tries to make Socrates agree to attempt to escape because he has been convicted by unjust laws. (T)

10. Plato gathered Socrates' writing and published them under his own name. (F)

11. In his later dialogues, Plato uses the character of Socrates as a mouthpiece for his own philosophy. (T)

12. Socrates believes there is a difference between opinion and knowledge. (T)

13. Both Socrates and Plato were engaged in a life-long intellectual battle in favor of the concept of ethical relativism. (F)

14. In Plato's dialogue *The Republic,* Socrates insists that only a well-balanced person with a sense of justice can be happy. (T)

15. For Plato the virtue of temperance is achieved when one's desires (appetites) are properly controlled. (T)

16. Both Plato and Freud developed theories that divided the human soul into three parts. (T)

17. Plato is considered the founder of modern Freudian psychoanalysis. (F)

18. Like Plato, Freud believes that we can access and control the part of the psyche that houses our desires and drives. (F)

19. Most philosophers who are interested in metaphysics are also believers in reincarnation. (F)

115

20. A metaphysical materialist is primarily interested in accumulating material goods. (F)

21. The world of Forms is unchangeable, according to Plato. (T)

22. The Forms are embedded in the world of things, according to Plato. (F)

23. In the "Myth of the Cave," the prisoners symbolize all people who are tied down by a sense of guilt. (F)

24. In the "Myth of the Cave," the prisoners symbolize all humans who think the world of the senses is the real world. (T)

25. Socrates was never given a chance to confront his accuser, Meletus, during his trial. (F)

26. Socrates says that "virtue is not given by money, but from virtue comes money and every other good of man, public as well as private." (T)

27. In *A Man for All Seasons*, Sir Thomas More is jailed and executed for heresy and corrupting the youth, in a historical situation bearing a remarkable resemblance to that of Socrates. (F)

28. In *A Man for All Seasons*, Sir Thomas More is jailed and executed for refusing to compromise his moral standards. (T)

29. In "The Store of the Worlds," Mr. Wayne fails the test of virtue by choosing to live a year in affluence and promiscuity. (F)

30. In "The Store of the Worlds," Mr. Wayne shows us what he thinks is the good life: The everyday life with his long-gone family. (T)

31. In *Cyrano de Bergerac*, Roxanne never realizes that it was Cyrano who wrote the love letters she cherished. (F)

Multiple-Choice Questions
(Correct answers are marked with an asterisk.)

32. Socrates gave several reasons why he did not want to attempt to escape from prison. Which one of these is the most likely one?
    a. because he believed that his sentence was just
    b. because he thought he could make a greater political impact by dying as a martyr
    c. because he was sick and was not able to stand up
    *d. because two wrongs wouldn't make a right

33. Why do people do morally wrong acts, according to Socrates?
    a. because human nature is evil
    *b. because people are ignorant
    c. because they haven't thought to ask themselves, "Could I want this to be a universal law?"
    d. because they haven't considered the consequences

34. A virtuous person must, according to Plato, be able to maintain a balance between the three parts of his or her psyche. Identify the one part that doesn't belong.
   *a. memory
   b. willpower
   c. appetites
   d. reason

35. Which virtue corresponds to which part of the psyche, according to Plato? (Only one pair is correctly matched.)
   a. Wisdom corresponds to willpower
   b. Courage corresponds to reason
   c. Temperance corresponds to memory
   *d. Courage corresponds to willpower

36. Freudian psychological theory involves three parts of the human psyche. Which one should not be on the list?
   a. Ego
   b. Superego
   *c. doxa
   d. Id

37. What is a "tripartite soul"?
   a. a person with multiple personality disorder
   b. a soul contemplating the problem of too much action, right action, and too little action
   *c. a soul consisting of three parts
   d. a person of multiple ethnic heritage

38. There are three major theories of metaphysics; identify the one that doesn't belong.
   a. materialism
   *b. realism
   c. idealism
   d. dualism

39. How do we learn about the Forms, according to Plato?
   a. by doing as much empirical research as possible
   b. by examining our emotions
   *c. by using our reason to recall the knowledge we had before we were born
   d. by reading the works of great philosophers

40. [Question #41 should only be used in a test that combines Chapters 8 and 9] Who speaks the following words? "For the fear of death is indeed the pretense of wisdom and not real wisdom, being a pretense of knowing the unknown; for no one knows whether death, which men in their fear think is the greatest evil, may not be the greatest good."
   *a. Socrates, in the *Apology*

b. Sir Thomas More, in *A Man for All Seasons*
c. Aristotle, in *Nicomachean Ethics*
d. Njal, in *Njal's Saga*

41. [Question #41 should only be used in a test that combines 8 and 9]
Who speaks the following words? "If we lived in a state where virtue was profitable, common sense would make us saints, but since we see that avarice, anger, pride and stupidity commonly profit far beyond charity, modesty, justice and thought, perhaps we must stand fast a little, even at the risk of being heroes."
a. Socrates, in the *Apology*
*b. Sir Thomas More, in *A Man for All Seasons*
c. Aristotle, in *Nicomachean Ethics*
d. Njal, in *Njal's Saga*

42. The theme of the noble soul trapped in a misunderstood body is featured in many stories. The textbooks mentions several. Which one of these is mentioned?
a. *The Three Musketeers*
b. *The Lion King*
*c. *Beauty and the Beast*
d. *Sense and Sensibility*

Essay/Study Questions

43. Heraclitus, a pre-Socratic philosopher, said, "Character is fate." What do you think he meant by this?

44. Why did Socrates refuse to leave Athens?

45. In your opinion, should Socrates have tried to escape? Why or why not?

46. What is Socrates' definition of the good life?

47. What did Socrates mean by saying that only ignorance leads to wrongdoing?

48. What are the three constitutive elements of the human person for Socrates/Plato? What is the proper relationship between these elements?

49. What are the Platonic Forms? Explain, using at least two examples. Why has Plato's philosophy led to calling him an idealist and/or dualist?

50. What do the Forms attempt to explain? What are some of the difficulties with Plato's theory of the Forms?

51. Explain the difference between materialism, idealism, and dualism, by using examples.

52. Tell the story of the Cave, and explain its philosophical significance.

53. What does Socrates mean by saying that if the Athenians put him to death, they will hurt themselves more than him?

54. Put yourself in the mind of one of the jurors at Socrates' trial. On the basis of the excerpt you've read, and the information you have from Chapter 8 about the conditions in Athens, what would your verdict be?

55. Imagine you were assigned as Socrates' legal counsel. What would you advise him to do or say in order to escape a death sentence? Do you think it might make a difference?

56. Explore the similarities and differences between the cases of Socrates and Sir Thomas More. If you were in More's position, what would you have chosen to do?

57. What is the meaning of the story of "The Store of the Worlds"?

58. Compare the story of Cyrano with other stories featuring the theme of "appearance vs. inner soul." Do they all have a Platonic message?

CHAPTER 9
Aristotle's Virtue Theory

True/False Questions

1. Aristotle was one of Socrates' most brilliant students. (F)

2. For Aristotle the Forms have no existence outside the world of things. (T)

3. The concept of teleology means a theory about the nature of God. (F)

4. According to Aristotle, everything has a function in the order of things, except fleas and snakes. (F)

5. We determine what a thing's purpose is by investigating what the thing in question does best. (T)

6. According to a teleological explanation, giraffes have long necks because of natural selection and mutation. (F)

7. According to a teleological explanation, giraffes have long necks so that they can reach high branches. (T)

8. To Aristotle, virtue means acting with excellence. (T)

9. Aristotle's virtue-theory says that there are three kinds of virtue: One which is in deficiency, one which is just right, and one which is in excess. (F)

10. For Aristotle we are morally good if we are capable of choosing the mean between extremes. (T)

11. Every action and emotion has a mean, a deficiency, and an excess. (T)

12. The virtue called proper pride has as its deficiency the vice humility and as its excess the vice prodigality. (F)

13. There is a discrepancy between Aristotle's list of virtues and vices and the Catholic list of cardinal virtues and sins. (T)

14. For Aristotle, true happiness is to be found in contemplation. (T)

15. The Catholic philosopher Saint Augustine relied greatly on the ideas of Aristotle. (F)

16. For Christian ethics, the moral rightness of following God's laws became more important than the belief in the human ability to shape one's own character. (T)

17. Aristotle was accused of the same crime as Socrates. (T)

18. For Aristotle, some virtues are closer to one extreme than the other. (T)

19. Christian scholars kept studying the works of Aristotle until he was rediscovered by Arab thinkers. (F)

20. Today the assumption that everything has a purpose is commonly accepted. (F)

21. For Christian ethics, the moral rightness of following God's laws became more important than the belief in the human ability to shape one's own character. (T)

22. According to Aristotle, there are some instances in which a brave man ought not to fear death. (T)

23. The brave man is, to Aristotle, a fearless man. (F)

24. In *Lord Jim*, Jim abandons ship with the rest of the crew during a storm, causing the death of hundreds of pilgrims. (F)

25. In *Njal's Saga*, Njal's wife and grandson choose to stay with him and are burned alive. (T)

26. In *Njal's Saga*, the little boy Thord is rescued at the last minute by Flosi's son. (F)

27. [Question #27 should only be used in a test combining Chapters 8 and 9] "The Flight of Icarus" is an excellent illustration of Plato's theory of Forms: The higher Icarus flies, the closer he gets to the Form of the good. (F)

28. "The Flight of Icarus" is an excellent illustration of Aristotle's theory of the golden mean. Since Icarus ignores his fathers advice to fly neither too high nor too low, he perishes. (T)

Multiple-Choice Questions
(Correct answers are marked with an asterisk.)

29. Aristotle's theory of causation includes four causes; identify the one that doesn't belong on the list.
    a. the material cause
    b. the final cause
    c. the formal cause
    *d. the ideal cause

30. According to Aristotle, if you have a deficiency of truthfulness, you are
    a. lying.
    b. being rude.
    c. virtuous.
    *d. using irony.

31. What is teleology?
    a. a theory about the nature of God
    *b. a theory that everything has a purpose
    c. a theory about the technology of broadcasting
    d. another word for *telemetry*

32. What does Aristotle mean by saying that "One swallow does not make a summer"?
    a. Do not believe what your eyes tell you.
    *b. Doing something virtuous once is not being virtuous; it must be done as a matter of habit.

c. You must wait until the time is ripe before acting; acting prematurely is a vice.

d. Do like the swallows; flee before the winds of winter.

33. The textbook asks three questions of Aristotle concerning his theory of virtue. Which one should not be included?

   a. If his theory is about character, why does he talk about actions and conduct?

   b. What does his list of virtues have to do with rational thinking?

   c. Must we do everything in the right amount, including lying, stealing, etc.?

   *d. Since he was a student of Plato, shouldn't the theory of Forms be featured more prominently?

34. Three girls are standing on a bridge, watching a small boy being swept downstream. Which virtue is this story an example of?

   a. honor

   *b. courage

   c. proper pride

   d. truthfulness

35. What is, to Aristotle, the ultimate form of human happiness?

   a. understanding the nature of God

   *b. habitually using one's reason during contemplation

   c. seeing one's children and grandchildren grow up

   d. being rich

36. During which time period did the West rediscover the writings of Aristotle?

   *a. during the Middle Ages

   b. during the Renaissance

   c. in the fourth century C.E.

   d. in the Nineteenth century

37. There are four major modern criticisms of the teleology of classical virtue-theory. Select the one that doesn't belong on the list.

   a. Must what is good for someone always be linked with what he or she does best?

   b. Why should rationality be the overriding purpose for humans?

   *c. Virtue-theory is undemocratic.

   d. Why should there be a purpose at all for human beings?

38. [Question #38 should only be used in a test combining Chapters 8 and 9] Who made the following statement? "With what sort of terrible things, then, is the brave man concerned? Surely with the greatest, for no one is more likely than he to stand his ground against what is awe-inspiring. Now death is the most terrible of all things; for it is the end, and nothing is thought to be any longer either good or bad for the dead. But the brave man would not seem to be concerned with death in all circumstances..."

   a. Socrates, in the *Apology*

b. Sir Thomas More, in *A Man for All Seasons*
*c. Aristotle, in *Nicomachean Ethics*
d. Bergthora, in *Njal's Saga*.

39. *Lord Jim* is a good example of applied virtue ethics, since the story examines the virtue of:
a. compassion.
b. gratitude.
*c. courage.
d. having a sense of humor.

40. In *Njal's Saga*, how do Njal and Bergthora choose to meet their deaths?
*a. They lay themselves down on the bed, while the house burns around them.
b. They try to fight off the flames as long as possible.
c. They rush out to meet Flosi and his men, weapon in hand, and are hacked down on their own doorstep.
d. They kneel down and pray until they succumb to smoke inhalation.

41. What is the origin of the story of Icarus?
a. Norse mythology
*b. Greek mythology
c. a Hollywood film from 1934
d. a novel by the German writer Goethe

Essay/Study Questions

42. What does the term "empiricism" mean? How does Aristotle's empiricism distinguish him from Plato?

43. What is Aristotle's doctrine of the four causes? What do they attempt to explain? How does it relate to his teleology?

44. What is the function, according to Aristotle, of a human being?

45. In the definition of virtue cited on page 295, what does it mean to say that "the mean relative to us . . . [is] determined by a rational principle by which the man of practical wisdom would determine it"? Who is this "rational man"?

46. What is the "mean" of Aristotle? Is it an arithmetic condition? Does it imply that the virtuous person is an average person, of average talents?

47. Explain Aristotle's theory of virtues, in detail, using at least three examples. At least two of the examples must be Aristotle's.

48. Explain the difference between a teleological explanation and a causal explanation by using examples.

49. Give an example of a virtue that is closer to one extreme than the other.

50. Evaluate Aristotle's idea that rationality is the overriding human purpose.

51. Describe your own criterion for moral goodness, and give an example of what *you* think is a morally good person. You may make up an example, or pick an actual or fictional person and describe him/her.

52. What constitutes happiness, or "eudaimonia," for Aristotle?

53. What are some of Rosenstand's criticisms of virtue ethics?

54. Is Jim (*Lord Jim*) a coward or is he courageous? Can one be both? According to Aristotle? According to you?

55. Would Aristotle consider Socrates' choice to stand trial a brave decision? Why or why not? Would he consider his own decision to flee Athens courageous? Why or why not?

56. How might Aristotle have evaluated Njal's and Bergthora's deaths? Explain.

57. Is "The Flight of Icarus" a didactic story? Explain.

CHAPTER 10
Modern Perspectives

True/False Questions

1. Virtue ethics claims that we are not responsible for the character and dispositions we are born with. (F)

2. There is a difference between a morality of virtue and an ethics of virtue. (T)

3. Virtue ethics believes that a negative role model cannot teach us anything about virtues; only a positive role model can. (F)

4. Bernard Mayo believes that a virtuous person usually does the right thing, but someone who follows moral rules of conduct may not always be a virtuous person. (T)

5. Kant believed that we learn virtue best from positive role models. (F)

6. Kant insisted that trying to learn virtue from role models does not lead to virtue, but to jealousy and resentment. (T)

7. Philippa Foot stresses that having a virtue is not the same as having a skill; it is having the proper intention. (T)

8. Foot claims that someone who is able to overcome his or her bad inclinations is a morally better person than someone who doesn't have bad inclinations. (F)

9. Christina Hoff Sommers believes that the proper way to teach values is to focus on Christian values of obedience and sexual abstinence. (F)

10. Sommers wants to teach students that values are not merely a matter of taste. (T)

11. Sommers believes that, in the end, moral problems such as pollution, the homeless, or the loneliness of elderly people must be solved by the state and not the individual. (F)

12. Søren Kierkegaard's father believed there was a curse on the family because he, as a child, had stepped on a loaf of bread to get across a mud puddle. (F)

13. Within the Lutheran tradition there is no confession and no absolution of sins by clergy. (T)

14. Kierkegaard shocked Romantic nineteenth-century Europe by claiming, a century ahead of his time, that "objectivity is truth." (F)

15. The character of Judge William is Kierkegaard's symbol of a person who is locked in the aesthetic stage. (F)

16. Heidegger calls humans "Being-There," because human existence is different than the existence of things and animals. (T)

17. Heidegger believes we ought to take into account what "they say," because forgetting about public opinion removes us from total existential awareness. (F)

18. Heidegger thinks humans feel anguish when they realize that all their concerns and rules are relative. (T)

19. Henri Bergson believes our true self will cause us to do unexpected things, but as long as we remain true to ourselves, we can't act in a morally wrong way. (F)

20. Bergson died from pneumonia caused by standing in line during the Nazi occupation of Paris to be registered as a Jew. (T)

21. Sartre's example of the young woman on a date is an example of Bad Faith. (T)

22. For Sartre all your choices count equally, even those you intended to make but never carried out. (F)

23. Nietzsche claims there are no absolute values, because God is dead. (F)

24. For Nietzsche a new moral value system must be advocated; one which respects the weaker individual and sets limits on the powers of the masters. (F)

25. For Erik Erikson a person with ego integrity is one who has never experienced an identity crisis. (F)

26. For Levinas, it is essential that we acknowledge that the Other and I are equal. (F)

27. For Levinas, religion no longer promises a happy ending; this means that ethics now has become the highest form of religious faith. (T)

28. Levinas has been criticized by feminists because he identifies the Other with woman. (T)

29. In his interview, Levinas makes it clear that ethics extends to all creatures with eyes that can look into yours, because anyone with a face becomes an Other. (F)

30. The drama No Exit features three people on Death Row awaiting their execution. (F)

31. In No Exit, Sartre claims that "Hell is other people." (T)

32. In Hannah and Her Sisters, Mickey almost kills himself and recaptures the meaning of life as a consequence. (T)

33. In A Few Good Men, Colonel Jessep admits to killing the soldier Santiago in a fit of rage over his incompetence. (F)

34. Babette (in Babette's Feast) spends her entire inheritance on cooking an elaborate meal for the congregation of the small village that took her in as a refugee. (T)

35. In *The Good Apprentice*, Edward is filled with guilt because he has caused the death of one of his friends. (T)

Multiple-Choice Questions
(Correct answers are marked with an asterisk.)

36. There are three major criticisms that one may raise against Mayo's idea of emulating role models. Which one shouldn't be on the list?
   a. What if your idea of a role model doesn't correspond to other people's role models?
   b. Merely imitating what someone else does is a life of inauthenticity.
   c. What if your role model turns out to be morally flawed?
   *d. Everyone is imperfect, so there really are no role models.

37. In her virtue theory, Philippa Foot shows a strong kinship with which philosopher?
   a. John Stuart Mill
   b. Plato
   *c. Aristotle
   d. Kierkegaard

38. Who speaks the following words? "It is wrong to mistreat a child, to humiliate someone, to torment an animal. To think only of yourself, to steal, to break promises."
   *a. Christina Hoff Sommers
   b. Jean-Paul Sartre
   c. Emmanuel Levinas
   d. Philippa Foot

39. Alasdair MacIntyre claims that virtue is linked to:
   a. the mean between extremes.
   *b. telling one's culture's traditional stories.
   c. social atomism.
   d. getting involved with the needs of one's community.

40. For Kierkegaard the phrase "subjectivity is truth" means the following:
   a. There is no objective knowledge, except for mathematical theorems.
   b. There is no objective knowledge, including mathematical theorems.
   *c. There is no objective truth about life, only a personal truth for each individual.
   d. Trick question: Kierkegaard says, "Objectivity is truth," and in this he is in agreement with most of the philosophical tradition.

41. Kierkegaard theorizes that there are three stages to the development of one's character. Which of the following is not one of the stages?
   a. the ethical stage
   *b. the existential stage
   c. the aesthetic stage
   d. the religious stage

42. What does Heidegger mean by saying that Being-Theres always care about something?
    a. No matter where you go, there you are, and then you have to deal with it.
    b. Humans are fundamentally moral beings, caring and compassionate.
    c. Any being who is self-aware is a compassionate being.
    *d. Humans are always engaged in something.

43. For Sartre, the belief that there is no God, and life is absurd, leads to the following conclusion:
    *a. Humans must create their own values through making choices.
    b. Everything is permissible, since there will be no eternal punishment.
    c. Since nothing has value, the life of the individual is worthless and human rights are nonexistent.
    d. There is no free will, since all of reality is a matter of material causes and effects.

44. What does Sartre mean by "Bad Faith"?
    a. being a bad Catholic
    b. trusting in someone who turns out to be untrustworthy
    *c. trying to avoid making a choice by pretending that you have no choice
    d. pretending that there is no god, but in your heart you really believe God exists

45. Someone who has ego integrity is:
    a. someone who has never undergone an identity crisis.
    b. someone who can be trusted in all business ventures.
    *c. someone who has an inner harmony and balance of the mind.
    d. someone who is proud of the fact that he or she cannot be bribed under any circumstances.

46. The theory of Friedrich Nietzsche that God is dead provides an early inspiration for which philosophy?
    a. Heidegger's theory that a closed-minded person is inauthentic
    *b. Sartre's theory that life is absurd, since there is no God
    c. Levinas's theory that the Other is more important than myself
    d. Kierkegaard's theory that an authentic human being must reach the religious stage

47. Which philosopher said, "Thus there are no accidents in a life; a community event which suddenly bursts forth and involves me in it does not come from the outside. If I am mobilized in a war, this war is *my* war; it is in my image and I deserve it."
    a. Heidegger
    b. Levinas
    c. Sommers
    *d. Sartre

48. Levinas says that "ethics precedes ontology." What does he mean?
    a. that a philosophy of existence comes before understanding the needs of the Other
    *b. that understanding the needs of the Other comes before a philosophy of existence
    c. that we understand the Other ever before we exist
    d. This is a trick question. In reality he says, "Ontology precedes ethics."

49. Three scholars/writers in this book have been mentioned in connection with the Biblical story of Abraham about to sacrifice his son. Which one shouldn't be on the list?
    a. Kierkegaard
    b. Levinas
    c. Kafka
    *d. Nietzsche

50. Which philosopher speaks the following words? "The approach to the face is the most basic mode of responsibility. As such, the face of the other is verticality and uprightness; it spells a relation of rectitude."
    *a. Levinas
    b. Sartre
    c. Sommers
    d. Kierkegaard

51. What does Levinas mean by saying that the alterity of the Other makes him or her my responsibility?
    a. The Other is different from me, but fundamentally equal, and that is why he or she is my moral responsibility.
    b. The Other is different from me, and psychologically less to me, because we are all selfish by nature. To control my selfish nature I must take him or her on as a moral responsibility.
    *c. The Other is different from me, and essentially more important than myself, so I must regard his or her needs as more important than my own.
    d. The Other is essentially the same as myself, and thus we are each other's responsibility.

Essay/Study Questions

52. Mayo wants us to emulate role models. Can you think of a person, either a historical figure, a living person, or a fictional character that you would like to emulate? Explain who, and why (or why not).

53. Discuss the issue of good disposition versus good conduct: Foot claims, with Aristotle, that a person who has a good disposition is slightly better than a person who has to control him or herself. Kant would say the opposite. Explain these viewpoints, and take sides: Which do you agree with, and why?

54. Discuss the story of Sommers's colleague whose students cheated on their ethics tests. Why did they cheat? Does the style and content of teaching ethics make a difference in terms of students cheating on tests, in your opinion?

55. Explain the relationship between Kierkegaard and his father, and the consequences it seems to have had for his philosophy.

56. In your opinion, does it make a difference for our reading of Heidegger that he was a member of the Nazi party? Why or why not?

57. What does Sartre mean by anguish? Explain, and give an example of how it feels and why it happens.

58. What does Sartre mean by saying we are condemned to be free?

59. Explain Sartre's concept of Bad Faith by using two examples: one of Sartre's and one of your own.

60. Discuss Levinas's view that the Other is more important than myself. What does he mean? Do you agree? Why or why not?

61. Levinas is reluctant to include animals as beings with "faces." Do you agree that ethics can be extended to animals only as a secondary move patterned after ethics toward humans, or should ethics toward animals be a primary form of ethics? Can Levinas's own theory be redesigned to include animals?

62. Describe the difference between fear and existential angst, on the basis of Mickey's experience in *Hannah and Her Sisters*.

63. How does Sartre's view of Hell in *No Exit* relate his view of dominance between individuals? What might Levinas comment on this play?

64. *A Few Good Men* argues that "I was just following orders" is never a good excuse. Relate this to Sartre's concept of bad faith and authenticity.

CHAPTER 11
Different Gender, Different Ethic?

True/False Questions

1. Feminism was originally associated with acquiring political and social rights for women. (T)

2. Modern feminism has a connection to virtue-ethics, in that modern feminists claim that only women can be truly virtuous. (F)

3. Impartiality and fairness are key concepts for modern feminism, since much of modern feminism is modeled after Rawls's theory of the original position. (F)

4. There is a strong movement in the academic world to get rid of gender-neutral language in favor of gender-specific language. (F)

5. The term *sexual dimorphism* means that the two sexes of a species look different, with one sex usually being larger than the other. (T)

6. Research has shown that women's sphere of influence has been historically limited to the private sector because they are biologically incapable of contributing significantly to the public sector. (F)

7. Some philosophers believe that women's rational capabilities don't measure up to those of men. (T)

8. Aristotle believed that the female is like a deformed male. (T)

9. Research has shown that men and women use their brains in exactly the same way, but come up with different results to the same questions. (F)

10. Rosenstand suggests that we should found our gender policy on actual, biological equality, rather than on a normative idea of equality. (F)

11. During the French Revolution, the issue of equal rights for women became one of the most important items on the agenda. (F)

12. Among women ethicists before the twentieth century are Mary Wollstonecraft, Harriet Taylor Mill, and Antoinette Brown Blackwell. (T)

13. Wollstonecraft argues that if the only thing girls are taught is how to seduce a man in order to acquire a husband, then they are not well equipped for married life. (T)

14. Mary Wollstonecraft was an eighteenth-century spokesperson for women's rights. (T)

15. John Stuart Mill was a nineteenth-century spokesperson for women's rights. (T)

16. Classical feminism was primarily concerned with the right for women to an equal share in the man's world. (T)

17. Classical feminism sees men and women as fundamentally different. (F)

18. One of the major events in the development of women's rights was World War I, when women had to take over men's work on the homefront. (T)

19. Simone de Beauvoir believes that if boys and girls are given a nonsexist education, they will become basically similar persons; gender differences are all a matter of environment. (T)

20. Monoandrogynism argues that homosexuality is preferable to heterosexuality. (F)

21. According to the Fair Employment and Housing Act, sexual harassment may consist of making or threatening reprisals after a negative response to sexual advances. (T)

22. According to the Fair Employment and Housing Act, sexual harassment may consist of uttering unsolicited complimentary remarks about an individual's clothes. (F)

23. An ultra-radical version of androgynism suggests changing human biology to eliminate gender differences. (T)

24. Scholars have pointed out that research into human nature has until recently focused on the male as the normal human being. (T)

25. Gilligan suggests that male and female moral values are fundamentally similar. (F)

26. Deborah Tannen suggests that men and women may find it hard to communicate because they grow up having different speech patterns. (T)

27. Christina Hoff Sommers identifies herself as a "gender feminist" in her book, *Who Stole Feminism?* (F)

28. In the excerpt from Gilligan's *In a Different Voice*, she refers to a fairy tale, "The Three Languages," as an illustration of the dynamics of male adolescence. (T)

29. In Ibsen's *A Doll's House*, Nora is in trouble because an old case of shoplifting has now resurfaced. (F)

30. Ibsen's *A Doll's House* can be seen as a harbinger of the modern debate about ethics of justice versus ethics of care. (T)

31. In *Like Water for Chocolate*, Tita must remain unmarried in order to take care of her mother, because she is the oldest daughter. (F)

32. Thelma and Louise start their downhill slide toward a life of crime because of Thelma's overdrawn credit card. (F)

Multiple-Choice Questions

(Correct answers are marked with an asterisk.)

33. Identify "sexual dimorphism":
    a. gender equality
    *b. one sex is larger than the other
    c. date rape
    d. sexual politics striving to maintain gender differences

34. Identify an early spokesperson in France for women's rights:
    *a. Poulain de la Barre
    b. Talleyrand
    c. Makrina of Neocaesaria
    d. Harriet Taylor

35. Who wrote, "I wish to persuade women to endeavor to acquire strength, both of mind and body, and to convince them that the soft phrases, susceptibility of heart, delicacy of sentiment, and refinement of taste, are almost synonymous with epithets of weakness"?
    a. John Stuart Mill
    b. Simone de Beauvoir
    *c. Mary Wollstonecraft
    d. Carol Gilligan

36. Simone de Beauvoir is, aside from being a feminist, also associated with which philosophical tradition?
    a. utilitarianism
    *b. existentialism
    c. Platonism
    d. Kantian deontology

37. Simone de Beauvoir claims that:
    *a. women and men have different patterns of behavior because of differences in upbringing.
    b. women and men have different patterns of behavior because of biological reasons.
    c. women and men have different patterns of behavior because of individual differences.
    d. women and men have fundamentally similar patterns of behavior.

38. The Fair Employment and Housing Act identifies several situations of sexual harassment. Which one shouldn't be on the list?
    a. unwanted sexual advances
    b. making or threatening reprisals after a negative response to sexual advances
    *c. uttering unsolicited complimentary remarks about an individual's clothes
    d. verbal abuse of a sexual nature

39. What is polyandrogynism?
    a. the same as monoandrogynism
    b. the same as homosexuality
    *c. the theory that gender roles should be left as open as possible
    d. the theory that men and women ought to share all the best qualities of the traditional gender roles

40. What is Heinz's dilemma?
    *a. Heinz's wife is sick, and he has no money for medication. Should he steal the drugs she needs?
    b. Heinz's wife has had an affair with another man, and he has to decide whether to file for divorce.
    c. Heinz's wife has stolen drugs. Should he tell the police?
    d. Heinz is in love with another woman. Should he tell his wife?

41. How does Gilligan evaluate Amy's solution to Heinz's dilemma?
    a. Amy is confused and has not understood that saving a life is more important than keeping the law.
    b. Amy is confused and has not understood that keeping the law is more important than saving a life.
    *c. Boys tend to think in terms of justice, and girls in terms of caring, and Jake's and Amy's answers are both right, each in their own way.
    d. Amy has understood the situation perfectly, and Jake has misunderstood everything, because men always misunderstand everything.

42. Who wrote this? "Thus women not only define themselves in a context of human relationships but also judge themselves in terms of their ability to care. Women's place in man's life cycle has been that of nurturer, caretaker, and helpmate, the weaver of those networks of relationships on which she in turn relies."
    a. Beauvoir
    b. Wollstonecraft
    c. Ibsen
    *d. Gilligan

43. In Ibsen's *A Doll's House*, what is the miracle Nora hopes for?
    a. that Krogstad is going to tear up her IOU
    b. that her father will recover from his illness
    *c. that Torvald will show his love by taking the blame for her forgery
    d. that Torvald will forgive her for her wrongdoing

44. In Esquivel's *Like Water for Chocolate*, someone tells of a theory about matches of passion inside every person. Who tells the story?
    a. Tita, to Gertrudis
    b. Nacha, to Tita
    *c. John Brown, to Tita
    d. Mama Elena, to all three daughters

45. What is the initial incident that propels Thelma and Louise on their journey toward crime and self-awareness?
    a. Louise is battered by her boyfriend, and kills him.
    *b. Thelma is the victim of attempted rape, and the attacker is killed by Louise.
    c. A truck driver shouts obscenities at them, and they set fire to his truck.
    d. Their cash is stolen by Thelma's lover, and they track him down and beat him up.

Essay/Study Questions

46. Discuss the theory that there is a connection between virtue-ethics and modern feminism. Wherein lies the connection?

47. Discuss the issue of sexual harassment. Are the guidelines provided by the Fair Employment and Housing Act reasonable? Why or why not? Should lawyers date their clients? Should doctors date their patients? Should professors date their students? Why or why not?

48. Give an example of a gender-specific expression, and substitute with a gender-neutral expression.

49. What does Beauvoir mean by saying that the only way for a woman to become authentic is to leave her role as "deviant"?

50. What is the difference between monoandrogyny and polyandrogyny?

51. In your view, are men and women fundamentally different or basically similar if given a nonsexist type of education? Your answer should include a brief description of Beauvoir's and Gilligan's theories.

52. Discuss Heinz's dilemma. Is Jake correct? Is Amy correct? Is Gilligan correct in her criticism? Is it fair to say that Amy should have understood what Kohlberg meant by his question?

53. Christina Hoff Sommers criticizes new feminists for making women into victims. Discuss her statements. Do they have any merit? Why or why not?

54. In Ibsen's *A Doll's House,* what is the miracle Nora expected? What is her reaction, when she realizes that it is not going to happen? Is it a reasonable or unreasonable reaction? Explain.

55. [Question #55 should only be given in a test combining Chapters 10 and 11]. Evaluate Gilligan's statement that "Sensitivity to the needs of others and the assumption of the responsibility for taking care lead women to attend to other voices than their own and to include in their judgment other points of view." What might Levinas (Chapter 10) comment on this statement?

56. Is Ibsen's *A Doll's House* a realistic representation of the way a woman would feel and react in Nora's situation? Of a man in Helmer's situation? Is Ibsen being fair to Helmer? Discuss Nora's statement that millions of women have sacrificed their honor for love.

57. Evaluate the characters in *Like Water for Chocolate*. Is anyone exhibiting an "ethic of care"? Explain.

58. The screenwriter of *Thelma and Louise*, Callie Khouri, is herself a well-known feminist writer. Is this a story of "classical feminism" or "new feminism"? How might Christina Hoff Sommers respond to this film?

CHAPTER 12
Virtues, Values, and Religion

True/False Questions

1. Confucius defines the man of virtue as someone wise, courageous, and with a good head for business. (F)

2. The Way is practiced by developing good habits and continual good thinking. (T)

3. Both Aristotle and Confucius believed that it is virtuous to practice moderation. (T)

4. Both Aristotle and Confucius believed in the Golden Rule as the essential moral approach to life. (F)

5. Mencius believed that humans are born morally neutral but are capable of developing toward being either morally good or evil. (F)

6. Mencius believed that in order to become truly virtuous you have to go through suffering. (T)

7. Taoism is a philosophy which advocates that the superior person must try to affect change in order to make life better for others. (F)

8. The concept of *wu-wei* is Taoism's concept for proper conduct: doing nothing. (T)

9. In Mahayana Buddhism there are numerous Buddhas. (T)

10. Buddhism advocates a renunciation of self-indulgence by way of asceticism and strict self-denial. (F)

11. The concept of karma is a system of reward and punishment for the soul after death. (F)

12. In Buddhism, karma is the force that binds the soul to a new reincarnation because of the accumulated results of past deeds and cravings. (T)

13. The Buddhist concept of suffering does not mean physical and mental suffering as much as impermanence or imperfection. (T)

14. Buddhism is an Asian system of virtue ethics, while Confucianism is an ethics of conduct. (F)

15. Plato has been highly influential in Islamic philosophy. (F)

16. The ideas of fatalism and the idea of free will are mutually supportive philosophies in Islam. (F)

17. In Islam, the true sin is disobedience toward Allah in the sense of forgetting His commands. (T)

18. According to Avicenna, woman's nature is weak and she must be protected from herself so that she will not cause dishonor to her husband. (T)

19. Islam sees the major moral problem as a problem of human character weakness. (T)

20. Within the history of Judaism there are traditions of ethics of conduct as well as of virtue ethics. (T)

21. The Jewish rule of charity is directed exclusively toward one's coreligionists. (F)

22. Modern Judaism has been continually interested in virtue-ethics, contrary to secular Western ethics. (T)

23. Levinas is by many readers considered a modern moral philosopher within the Jewish tradition. (T)

24. Levinas agrees with Martin Buber that "I" and "Thou" should be viewed as fundamentally equal. (F)

25. Augustine did not become a Christian until he was a mature scholar. (T)

26. Thomas Aquinas did not become a Christian until he was a mature scholar. (F)

27. For Augustine, all human beings are tainted by the original sin. (T)

28. Thomas Aquinas was heavily influenced by the writings of Aristotle. (T)

29. The divine command theory states that God has commanded the moral law because it is right. (F)

30. The divine command theory states that the moral law is right because God commands it. (T)

31. The Viking values include the following: Justice among equals, loyalty among family and friends, and mercy and generosity toward strangers and enemies. (F)

32. The Akan people of Ghana believe humans can acquire a good character through listening to stories. (T)

33. The moral system of the Akan people forms a link between ethics of conduct and virtue-ethics, according to scholar Kwame Gyekye. (T)

34. The Native American values include an understanding that humans have only a small part to play in the general order of things. (T)

35. The ecologist Callicott sees the Native American value system as one based on social interaction between members of the entire natural world. (T)

36. The ecologist Callicott sees the Native American value system as one based on mutual cooperation and storyswapping among tribes of humans, to the exclusion of the rest of the environment. (F)

37. The excerpt from Confucius shows that he was teaching the negative rule, "Do not do unto others what you would not have done unto you," and not the positive, Golden Rule. (F)

38. Confucius teaches to "Love your enemies, do good to them which hate you. Bless them that curse you, and pray for them which despitefully use you." (F)

39. The Viking tradition teaches that "Cattle die, kindred die, ever man is mortal; but the good name never dies of one who has done well." (T)

40. A Native American proverb says that, "The prosperity of man depends upon his fellow man." (F)

41. In the Syrian folktale, "Test of Friendship," a father is accused of killing a sheep, but his son comes to his aid in the last minute. (F)

42. In Singer's "A Piece of Advice," Baruch's father-in-law is told by a rabbi to pretend to be a peaceful, humble man. (T)

43. In the African folktale, "The Quality of Friendship," a young man must kill his son to save his friend from being eaten by a snake. (F)

44. In the Lakota Sioux story of White Buffalo Woman, a young woman visits the Lakota people and teaches them that killing the buffalo is wrong, because buffalo are persons, too. (F)

Multiple-Choice Questions
(Correct answers are marked with an asterisk.)

45. Confucius identifies a man of virtue as someone with the following three characteristics. Which of the following is not one of those characteristics?
    a. wisdom
    *b. a good head for business
    c. courage
    d. humaneness

46. Which view is Mencius's own view of human nature?
    a. There is no such thing as human nature.
    b. There are those who are good by nature, and there are those who are evil by nature, but proper guidance can set anybody straight.
    *c. Human nature is good from the beginning, and will remain good if guided right.
    d. Human nature is morally neutral from birth, and it can become good or bad.

47. What is the most important duty, according to Mencius?
    a. the duty toward one's children
    b. the duty toward the state
    *c. the duty toward one's parents
    d. the duty toward one's spouse

48. Gautama received three jolts to his complacency that were to change his life and cause him to found the philosophy of Buddhism. Which of the following is not one of those jolting experiences?
    a. the experience of age

b.   the experience of death
c.   the experience of disease
*d.   the experience of poverty

49.   Which of the following is not one of the Four Noble Truths that Buddhism is based on?
a.   Suffering is caused by craving.
*b.   The way to stop life is to meditate on one's cravings.
c.   If cravings stop, suffering will stop, too.
d.   Life is suffering.

50.   The Buddhist must, aside from living according to the Noble Eightfold Path, also pay attention to five everyday rules. Find the one that doesn't belong on the list.
a.   Do not kill.
b.   Do not commit adultery.
c.   Do not speak falsely.
*d.   Do not disgrace your father and mother.

51.   The Qur'an lists five classes of human actions. Which one shouldn't be on the list?
a.   acts that are commanded
b.   acts that are forbidden
c.   acts that are not permitted in formal worship
*d.   acts that are not permitted in informal trade relations

52.   The Jewish doctrine of ethical monotheism has four components. Which one doesn't belong?
a.   God's laws are binding on everyone in society, even the privileged classes.
*b.   The moral standards apply to everyone, except God, since He is all-powerful.
c.   God's laws protect everyone in society, especially the underprivileged.
d.   The moral standards apply to everyone, including God.

53.   Maimonides sees four levels of personal growth. Identify the highest level.
a.   the level of everyday life and material possessions
b.   the level of moral virtue, developed by good habits
c.   the level of physical fitness, good health, and an even temper
*d.   the level of rational virtue, developed by understanding God

54.   Which tradition expresses these ethical rules: "Be considerate of the feelings of a poor man, by giving him alms in secret, and on no account before others. For this reason also give him food and drink in your own house—but do not watch him while he is eating"?
a.   the Chinese tradition
*b.   the Jewish tradition
c.   the Viking tradition
d.   the Islamic tradition

140

55. What is, in the Christian tradition, the *original sin?*
    *a. the disobedience of Adam and Eve in the Garden of Eden
    b. the first time in his or her life that a child disobeys his or her parents
    c. the same as Freud's concept of the pleasure principle
    d. the first murder: the killing of Abel by his brother Cain

56. From which tradition comes this quote? "For the person ... is not a palm tree that he or she should be complete or self-sufficient."
    a. the Viking tradition
    *b. the Akan tradition
    c. the Jewish tradition
    d. the Muslim tradition

57. From which tradition comes this quote? "And what, monks, is the Noble Truth of Suffering? Birth is suffering, aging is suffering, death is suffering..."
    a. The Confucian tradition
    b. The Christian tradition
    c. The Jewish tradition
    *d. The Buddhist tradition

58. From which tradition comes this quote? "Like the Most-High-Power-Whose-Ways-Are-Beautiful Boy he goes forth. All is beautiful behind him. All is beautiful before him."
    *a. the Native American tradition
    b. the Akan tradition
    c. the Viking tradition
    d. the Confucian tradition

59. The Akan people's view of human nature is:
    a. that people are born intrinsically good and become corrupted by bad influence.
    *b. that people are born morally neutral and become good by developing good habits.
    c. that people are born intrinsically evil and must be redeemed through their religious belief.
    d. that some are born good and some are born evil, as a matter of fate.

Essay/Study Questions

60. At the beginning of Chapter 12, two (possibly universal) rules of moral behavior are listed: "Do not harm the innocent (of your own culture)," and "Be respectful of the people in authority (who might harm you)." How does the logic of these maxims differ? What sort of justifications are offered?

61. Why would ethical systems be so closely tied to religious tradition throughout so much of human history? Why is that fact often a controversial one in our current "values" debate?

62. Why is it that so many of the detailed traditions in Chapter 12 focus on the figure of the virtuous individual as the exemplar of the moral life?

63. What are the similarities and differences between Confucius and Aristotle?

64. Why is it not enough for Mencius that one complete a moral duty? What else is required? How does this compare to Aristotle's recognition that one can act virtuously without being virtuous? Compare this with the narrative by Isaac Singer about the father-in-law who learns to be virtuous.

65. According to Buddha, what is the source of human suffering? What is the solution? Do you consider this feasible or rational?

66. For those who believe in God's omniscience there is a problem reconciling this idea with the idea of human free will. Explain the problem.

67. Discuss the fundamentalist Islamic custom of protecting women from the world as well as from themselves by keeping them in seclusion.

68. What are the four levels of perfection according to Maimonides?

69. Compare them to Kierkegaard's theory of the three stages in Chapter 10. What are the differences? What are the similarities?

70. Identify the tradition of the quote, "Love your enemies, do good to them which hate you." Discuss the meaning and merit of the excerpt.

71. Explain the difference between divine command theory and natural law.

72. Discuss the saying from *Havamal:* "Cattle die, kindred die, you yourself will die. What never dies is the good name you have won for yourself." Do you agree? Can such a saying apply to our own age?

73. If we recognize loyalty as a moral virtue, how might it cause a moral conflict for an individual? Consider this in light of the Viking code of ethics.

74. Evaluate the environmentalist values of Native American philosophy. Can they be used in the world of today? Why or why not?

75. What is the relationship between storytelling and the moral exemplar in tribal cultures?

76. Identify the traditions that emphasize the importance of community, and discuss their similarities and differences.

77. Write an essay, paraphrasing all excerpts in modern language, and comment on their advice, their similarities and differences.

78. How can the story of "Test of Friendship" be seen to illustrate the danger of a weak character?

79. Comment on "A Piece of Advice": (1) Is this an example of virtue ethics or ethics of conduct? (2) Can someone become a better person through consistent actions, even if his or her character is quite different?

80. Compare "The Quality of Friendship" with the Akan tradition of storytelling. How might this story serve as a didactic lesson for the young?

81. Discuss the moral lesson of "White Buffalo Woman" using Callicott's statement about Native Americans and their attitude toward the environment.

CHAPTER 13
Case Studies in Virtue

True/False Questions

1. Thomas Hobbes and Jean-Jacques Rousseau agreed that humans are naturally compassionate toward each other. (F)

2. Mencius and Rousseau agreed that humans are good by nature but have been corrupted by the circumstances of life. (T)

3. For Philip Hallie, institutionalized cruelty has the psychological effect that the victim comes to believe the cruelty is justified. (T)

4. Hallie believes that the best antidote against institutionalized cruelty is to show kindness to the victim. (F)

5. Hallie believes that it is better to have compassion, even if you cause death and destruction, than not to have any compassion at all. (F)

6. For Richard Taylor reason has no role to play in moral matters; all one needs is compassion. (T)

7. Taylor's three stores of atrocities show that what counts are the dreadful consequences of these acts, not the intentions behind them. (F)

8. The film *Forrest Gump* is seen by some critics as an example of a dangerous overemphasis on the moral powers of the intellect. (F)

9. In *Huckleberry Finn,* Huck helps the runaway slave Jim, and Jonathan Bennett thinks Huck is doing the wrong thing. (F)

10. Nobody can demand gratitude from us because gratitude is a feeling we cannot control. (F)

11. Lin Yutang's main point is criticizing the West for being indifferent toward our children and homeless people. (F)

12. Lin Yutang believes we owe a debt of gratitude to our parents for having raised us. (T)

13. Jane English uses the "debt-metaphor" to advocate the idea that grown children owe a debt to their parents for raising them. (F)

14. There are appropriate ways of using the debt-metaphor, according to English, and describing favors between strangers is one of them. (T)

15. For English there are only duties when there are favors, but there are no duties or obligations between friends. (F)

16. Fred Berger believes that in order to determine the amount of gratitude one ought to show, one must look at the giver's intentions. (T)

17. English believes that all dating problems would be solved if both parties would agree at the outset that the date is, basically, a business agreement. (F)

18. English suggests that parents ought to say to their grown children, "If you love us, you'll do X." (T)

19. The linguist Deborah Tannen claims that the Golden Rule doesn't work when people have different visions of correct behavior. (T)

20. The vice of excess corresponding to compassion is cold-heartedness. (F)

21. The following is an ancient Greek proverb: "Vengeance is mine, saith the Lord." (F)

22. While showing gratitude is something many must learn, receiving gratitude is not difficult at all. (F)

23. Rosenstand claims that just like it takes skill to be a good giver, so it takes skill to be a good receiver. (T)

24. Lin Yutang claims that a cultural man loves his children, but a natural man loves his parents. (F)

25. The parable of the Good Samaritan is an example of a didactic story. (T)

26. The Good Samaritan is the story of a man in ancient Israel who stopped to help an accident victim and was himself mugged by thieves. (F)

27. King Yudisthira refused to enter the gates of Heaven, because the god Indra wouldn't let his old dog in. (T)

28. King Yudisthira refused to enter the gates of Heaven, because his old dog growls, and alerts his master that it really is the gate to Hell. (F)

29. In *Schindler's List*, Schindler is a Jew who narrowly escapes death in Nazi Germany and makes a list of Nazi war criminals to be tracked down and taken to justice after the war. (F)

30. In the film *Eat Drink Man Woman*, Mr. Chu finally marries Mrs. Liang because she is such a good cook. (F)

31. In the film *Grand Canyon* Simon saves Mack from being a victim of gang violence, but receives no thanks in return. (F)

32. Othello is jealous of his wife because he suspects her of having an affair with his friend Cassio. (T)

33. The moral lesson of *Othello* is that women can't be trusted: They are by nature promiscuous. (F)

34. In "The Faithful Wife and the Woman Warrior," Blue Hawk's wife has an affair with Red Hawk, and in anger Blue Hawk drowns her in the river. (F)

35. The Count of Monte Cristo is bent on revenge until he realizes that he has been wrong in assuming that he was the hand of God. (T)

36. In the film *The Searchers*, Ethan wants to kill his niece Debbie because he believes she has been contaminated by living with the Comanche Indians. (T)

144

37. What is institutionalized cruelty, according to Philip Hallie?
    a. cruelty committed by personnel in institutions such as boarding schools, orphanages, nursing homes, and hospitals
    *b. a systematic physical and psychological breakdown of victims by victimizers
    c. a systematic physical and psychological breakdown of an individual by members of an institution such as a school or a military academy
    d. cruelty elevated to an art where the physical signs are invisible

38. Imagine you come across a seven-year-old child torturing a puppy. There are several possible arguments you might use that are aimed at dissuading someone from hurting someone else. Which one might Taylor advocate?
    *a. Appeal to his or her compassion: "How do you think the puppy feels?"
    b. Appeal to his or her sense of universalizability: "What if everyone acted like you?"
    c. Appeal to his or her sense of consequences: "You won't get away with it, you know!"
    d. Appeals are a waste of time. Call the police, and in the meantime restrain the kid, not too gently.

39. What is Bennett's argument against Huck Finn?
    a. It was wrong of Huck to help a slave escape because in his day and age slaves were property, and ethical relativism dictates that one must follow the rules of one's society.
    *b. Huck did the right thing, but for the wrong reason: He should have found good reasons for helping Jim rather than just follow his instinct.
    c. Huck did the wrong thing, because he should have pleaded with Jim's owner to free him and not take matters into his own hands.
    d. Huck did the right thing, and Bennett doesn't argue against him at all—trick question.

40. According to Jane English, what kind of obligations do we have toward our parents?
    a. We have no obligations at all, because we didn't ask to be born.
    b. We have an obligation to love them, even if they haven't shown us love.
    c. We have unending obligations, because we owe them everything, since they raised us.
    *d. We have obligations according to their need and our ability to help, as long as there is friendship.

41. According to Berger, we must make certain that three factors are in place in order to find out whether we owe a debt of gratitude to someone. Which one shouldn't be on the list?
    a. We must find out if the favor was done for our own sake.
    b. We must find out if we were helped on purpose.
    c. We must find out if the help was given voluntarily.
    *d. We must find out if the favor was too generous.

42. What would be the vice of deficiency corresponding to the virtue of compassion?
    a. being intrusive
    *b. being cold-hearted
    c. being ungrateful
    d. feeling perpetually indebted

43. Which religious tradition claims the following? "Vengeance is mine, saith the Lord."
    a. the Buddhist tradition
    *b. the Judeo-Christian tradition
    c. the ancient Greek tradition
    d. the Confucian tradition

44. Identify a Chinese saying quoted by Lin Yutang:
    a. "One hand washes the other."
    b. "Vengeance is mine, saith the Lord."
    *c. "Water flows downwards and not upwards."
    d. "Go and do Thou likewise."

45. King Yudisthira refused to enter the gates of Heaven. Why?
    a. Since his old dog growled, he knew it was not really Heaven, but Hell.
    *b. Because he couldn't bring his old dog along.
    c. Because he was told that his wife had not been allowed to enter when she died.
    d. Because he was not dead yet.

46. Why did Schindler (*Schindler's List*) originally hire Jews in his factory?
    a. to save them from the death camps
    b. because they were particularly good workers
    c. because he was Jewish himself
    *d. for profit

47. What is "Schindler's List"?
    a. a list of Nazi war criminals, compiled by the Jewish avenger Schindler
    *b. a list of Jewish workers compiled by Schindler in order to save them from the Nazi death camps
    c. a list of Jewish workers compiled by the Nazi Schindler to be sent to the death camps
    d. a wishing list, given by Schindler to his girlfriend before Christmas.

48. What does the film *Eat Drink Man Woman* illustrate? Select the most likely answer.
    a. English's theory that grown children owe their parents nothing
    *b. the Asian tradition of the duty of taking care of one's parents
    c. the Asian tradition of the duty of the youngest daughter to stay unmarried in order to take care of her parents
    d. Taylor's theory that compassion comes from the heart, not the brain

49. What does *Grand Canyon* illustrate?
   *a. the question of how to give and receive gratitude
   b. the question of how to show compassion
   c. the question of how never to treat any rational being as merely a means to an end
   d. the vice of jealousy

50. Why is Othello jealous of his wife, Desdemona?
   *a. His enemy, Iago, has hinted that she is having an affair.
   b. His enemy, Iago, is having an affair with her.
   c. He is jealous of everyone she has known before she met him, including Iago.
   d. She is having an affair with his friend Cassio.

51. In *The Searchers*, Ethan is searching for his niece Debbie for eight years. What does he intend to do when he finds her?
   a. He wants to show his compassion to the orphaned girl by adopting her.
   b. He wants Marty to marry her.
   c. He wants to bring her home to her father and mother.
   *d. He wants to kill her.

Essay/Study Questions

52. Define Hallie's concept of institutionalized cruelty: (1) What kind of cruelty is it? (2) Why does it happen? and (3) What is the antidote?

53. Explain the Nazi Major's answer to the judge questioning his commitment to Nazism while allowing the escape of the refugees—"No, I believe in Nazism—but I could not stand by and watch innocent blood be shed." What might this example say about a conflict between political and moral commitments? Is there any virtue to intellectual and moral inconsistency?

54. What is Taylor trying to say with his stories of malice and goodness? Explain by referring to the stories.

55. What does the Huck Finn story reveal about the necessity of reason and compassion in ethical action?

56. Contrast the conclusions of Lin Yutang and Jane English on the parent-child relationship.

57. Contrast the metaphors of friendship and debt in relationships.

58. What is the difference between reciprocity and mutuality in English's theory? Explain with examples.

59. Discuss the issue of dating: A favor-debt situation or a friendship situation? Is there a way to resolve the problem of different expectations for dating partners in the future?

60. Why does Rosenstand argue that ethical pluralism is "probably the only viable solution for a future theory of ethics"?

61. Explain the quote, "Water runs downwards and not upwards."

62. Discuss the parable of the Good Samaritan on the basis of the university study mentioned in study question #3: Do you think you would be more inclined to stop and help if you remembered this story? Why or why not?

63. Evaluate the moral lesson of King Yudisthira and the dog. Is he being virtuous? Why or why not?

64. Discuss the quote from *Schindler's List*, taken from the Talmud, "Whoever saves one life saves an entire world." Compare the story of Schindler's list with Hallie's account of Le Chambon. Are there significant similarities and differences?

65. Describe the Confucian elements in the film *Eat Drink Man Woman*.

66. Discuss Mack's attempts to show gratitude in *Grand Canyon*, and Simon's willingness to receive gratitude.

67. On the basis of *Othello* and "The Faithful Wife and the Woman Warrior," discuss whether jealousy is ever an appropriate response. Explain your viewpoint.

68. On the basis of *The Count of Monte Cristo* and/or *The Searchers*, discuss whether thirst for revenge is ever an appropriate response. Explain your viewpoint.

CHAPTER 14
Conclusion: The Moral Importance of Stories

True/False Questions

1. The Russian author Ilya Ehrenburg read the diary of a young girl during World War II and became convinced that the Russians won the war because they kept meticulous diaries. (F)

2. In Bradbury's story *Fahrenheit 451* a group of book lovers memorize books of world literature, and each becomes a living book. (T)

3. Martha Nussbaum agrees with most of the philosophical tradition when she says that emotions have no cognitive value. (F)

4. For Nussbaum we understand ourselves and our emotions best through narratives. (T)

5. For Nussbaum it is inevitable that since narratives reflect the values of society, narratives deprive people of their moral autonomy. (F)

6. Soft universalism does not allow for a criticism of the stories of one's own culture. (F)

7. Rosenstand claims that empathy provoked by a story are building blocks of one's character. (T)

8. Ursula LeGuin believes that telling stories is a form of life denial. (F)

9. In *Star Trek: Voyager*, "Prime Factor," the crew of the *Voyager* tries to buy technology, offering the content of their library in return. (T)

10. In *Haroun and the Sea of Stories*, the evil ruler Khattam-Shud attempts to eliminate storytelling because storytelling is uncontrollable. (T)

Multiple-Choice Questions
(Correct answers are marked with an asterisk.)

11. What is Narrative Time?
    a. the time it takes to tell a story
    b. the time period in which a historical or contemporary novel is set
    c. the age of oral storytelling before writing was invented
    *d. the compressed time experience of a novel or a film

12. Who says that "novels preserve mystery and indeterminacy"?
    *a. Martha Nussbaum
    b. Ursula LeGuin
    c. Salman Rushdie
    d. Captain Janeway, in *Star Trek: Voyager*

13. The textbook tells of a story about a man who got what he wished for: a life like in the movies. What was his experience?
    a. He was incapable of dying, like a cartoon figure.
    b. He found himself to be a victim in a horror movie.
    *c. He lived his whole life in two hours.
    d. He never had to go to the bathroom.

14. The textbook compares the *Star Trek: Voyager* episode "Prime Factor" with another story from the textbook. Which one?
    a. *Blade Runner*
    b. *Pulp Fiction*
    c. "The Jigsaw Man"
    *d. *Star Trek: The Next Generation,* "Justice"

15. [Question #15 should only be used in a test that combines Chapters 13 and 14] Who says, "What's the use of stories that aren't even true?"
    *a. Khattam-Shud in *Haroun and the Sea of Stories*
    b. Tuvok in "Prime Factor"
    c. Goeth, in *Schindler's List*
    d. Martha Nussbaum

Essay/Study Questions

16. What is "Narrative Time"? Explain by using an example.

17. Nussbaum claims that philosophy has not wanted to deal with emotions because when humans are emotional, they are not self-sufficient. What does she mean by that?

18. Comment on Nussbaum's statement: "We have never lived enough. Our experience is, without fiction, too confined and too parochial. Literature extends it, making us reflect and feel about what might otherwise be too distant for feeling."

19. Consider Ehrenburg's statement about books. Do you think that knowing good stories might have survival value? Why or why not?

20. Consider the multicultural challenge of storytelling. Do you know any story that has made you understand another culture better? Do you know any story from your own tradition that expresses ideas you find it hard to accept? Do you know any story from another cultural tradition expressing ideas that you find hard to accept? Is it possible to find some common ground? Explain.

21. Would you agree with the statement in *Star Trek: Voyager* that noble stories can affect our lives the most? Explain. Do you know any stories that might qualify as "noble"?

22. Identify the narrative with the statement, "What's the use of stories that aren't even true," and discuss the idea that stories have an element that can't be controlled. Does the author consider that a positive or a negative thing? How do you feel about it?